SITES OF DISQUIET

The Non-Space in Spanish American Short Narratives and Their Cinematic Transformations

Ilka Kressner

I0893946

Purdue University Press
West Lafayette, Indiana

∞ The paper used in this book meets the minimum requirements of American National Standard for Information Sciences—Permanence of Paper for Printed Library Materials, ANSI Z39.48-1992.

Printed in the United States of America
Template for interior design by Anita Noble;
template for cover by Heidi Branham.
Cover photo: Film clip from *La cifra impar*, dir. Manuel Antin, Norma Vigo, 1962. Reproduced with permission of the director, Universidad del Cinema, Buenos Aires, Argentina.

Library of Congress Cataloging-in-Publication Data

Kressner, Ilka, 1975–
Sites of disquiet : the non-space in Spanish American short narratives and their cinematic transformations / Ilka Kressner.
pages cm. — (Purdue Studies in Romance Literatures ; Volume 58)
Includes bibliographical references and index.
ISBN 978-1-55753-654-9 (pbk. : alk. paper) — ISBN 978-1-61249-287-2 (epdf) — ISBN 978-1-61249-288-9 (epub) 1. Spanish American fiction—20th century—History and criticism. 2. Spanish American literature—Film adaptations. 3. Personal space in literature. 4. Space and time in literature. 5. Sacred space in literature. 6. Space (Architecture) in literature. I. Title.
PQ7082.N7K68 2013
863'.60998—dc23

2013016009

For my parents and Mumi

Contents

Preface

Approaching Un-common Grounds

Fernando Vidal Olmos, the paranoid and lonesome investigator of a mysterious sect of the blind in Ernesto Sábato's *Sobre héroes y tumbas* (*On Heroes and Tombs*) [1959], relates his encounter with a strange force: "Temía que el mundo que me rodeaba pudiera empezar a moverse, … a disgregarse, a transformarse, a perder todo sentido. … Mi propio yo empezaba de pronto a deformarse, a estirarse" (254–55). In the context of Spanish American *nueva narrativa* or Boom writings, Fernando is not alone in facing such a disquieting site of potentiality that threatens to transgress the edges of his body and disturbs his intellectual faculties. Many works from that period engage in experiments with liminal spaces that become active forces in the narrative universes. Although the body of criticism on the *nueva narrativa* works is among the most ingenious and copious in Spanish American literary studies, the analysis of space has not received the same amount of critical attention as have studies of metaphysical and existentialist questions, the conception of language, the role of perception, and, more recently, the portrayal of time.

In the pages to follow, I propose to analyze the portrayals of space in writings by Jorge Luis Borges, Julio Cortázar, Juan Rulfo, and Gabriel García Márquez. The sites in many of their texts are bizarre, yet differently from Latin American *novelas de la tierra* or from fiction in the high modernist vein, which were the predecessors and sources of inspiration for the Spanish American authors. No other devouring jungle annihilates the characters as does the one in José Eustasio Rivera's *La vorágine* (*The Vortex*) [1924]; no other impassible, dark quarry echoes the protagonist's existential angst as does the one in Franz Kafka's *The Trial* (1925). In many works by *nueva narrativa* authors, the characters face shifting perspectives or find themselves in inscrutable surroundings that extend beyond clearly discernible confines.[1] Their reaction toward such sites is of a constant spatial and corporeal unease. For instance, in Julio Cortázar's "Lejana: Diario de Alina Reyes" (*Bestiario*; "The Distances," *Bestiary*) [1951], space moves the characters as if they were its marionettes. The protagonist living in Buenos

Aires experiences a fatal spatial attraction for a bridge in Budapest that makes her travel to the Hungarian capital, embrace a beggar she meets at that bridge, and switch spirits with her. In Borges's "El Sur" (*Ficciones*; "The South," *Fictions*) [1956], space even becomes a character in itself, when the personified South throws a dagger to the perplexed anti-hero Dahlman, urging him to fight. The puzzling and vague topographic allusions do not fit into any known category of literary representation of space. Neither sites of projection (as *utopia* or *dystopia*) nor neutral, comprehensible settings (as the *topos*), the spaces under exposure are real; yet, also, elusive and transforming. In contrast to the inhabitants of fantastic worlds, the occupants of these spaces do not accept them as a spatial given, but are constantly on their guard. This alternative "non-space" imposes its presence indirectly. Its ambiguity, translated through a resistance to being rendered in a conventional manner, underwrites the questioning of common premises in the production and perception of space.

As a result of the pivotal role of spatiality and visual imagery in these texts, they have readily lent themselves to cinematic adaptation. Since the late 1960s, Latin America has seen a wave of filmic translations on the subject matter of a "non-space" and experimentation with alternative spatialities.[2] In the face of the ensuing challenges, I engage in an intermedial study of five literary works and seven of their adaptations to the screen. From a methodological point of view, the construction of space can best be studied in works—whether literary or cinematographic—in which it is no longer the taken-for-granted environment for action, but part of the action itself. Toward this end, I explore the spaces in my sources not as mere metaphors but as literary and cinematographic realities that question the characters', and indirectly, even our own everyday ideas of time-space, displacement, orientation, and mental mapping. This focus brings literature and philosophy of space into a dialogue with anthropological and psychoanalytical approaches. I will mostly draw on the concept of *atopos* or "non-space," developed by Roland Barthes, Michel de Certeau, and Marc Augé; on Paul Virilio's analyses of spaces of mobility; on Carlos Alonso's notion of the "in-between"; on the study of sites of self-effacing presence according to Jacques Derrida; and of echoing silences, based on Gayatri Spivak's elaborations.

Why does such a specific spatiality become an eminent feature in the different literary texts and films? No doubt, the reasons for the recurrence of the theme in variation are diverse. For instance in Sábato's texts, written right after Juan Domingo Perón's seizure of power, the disquieting spaces translate a heightened awareness of the underlying repression of the proclaimed transparent and just political system. The vague psychic and social disquiet is conveyed through space, a paradigmatic entity that brings the individual and the political together. In Gabriel García Márquez's short stories, the divergent practices of space transmit a critique of a neocolonial mindset. In the case of the spaces of Mozambique-born Brazilian director Ruy Guerra, the elusive spaces counter discourses of repressive nationalisms. Beyond these idiosyncratic motivations to develop artistic alternative spaces, the common motivation in all works, I argue, is an endeavor to surmount the dissatisfaction with a belief system, based on the primacy of the concisely defined abstract word over the disordered material world, and a shift from the text toward the (spatial) context.

The common theme of the literary and filmic works correlates with one of the main arguments of poststructural thought, according to which language is structured by absence. Art becomes a field of experimentation with spaces of absence, hence with spatial assumptions, conceptions, and practices, parallel to theoretical models. While Foucault and Derrida highlight the constructedness and slipperiness of language and concepts in relation to the world, the Spanish American artists proceed in an inverse fashion and detect a slipperiness of the apparently commonplace surroundings, which may lead to equally deep revisions of the human faculty to understand and put the world into words. I see a common liberating impetus in the theoretical and artistic approaches to words and spaces of vagueness, plurality, and absence. Their openness allows for more individualized and creative interactions with them, and enables relations where volatility ceases to be a negative value.

Sábato's Fernando Vidal Olmos dies in a frantic pursuit because, according to him, he does not succeed in "mantener la realidad en su sitio y en su forma" (255). Not all encounters with the "non-space" are as drastic. Those characters who take the moving surroundings as instances to be reckoned with, and those who interact with them in a less rigid way (as do several of the protagonists in the following chapters) learn to carve out a more individual and relieved narrative or filmic existence within the "non-space."

In my selection of disquieting space-fictions, I explore some of the most diverse and extreme cases in the works belonging to the Boom narratives and their filmic versions, and I examine the literary and cinematic strategies to convey them, such as the portrayal of spaces of total darkness, of absence, multi-layered sites, spaces that are only filled with echo, or radical *atopoi* of dispersion. I read Jorge Luis Borges's short story "Hombre de la esquina rosada" ("Man on Pink Corner") [1933] as the initial example of a portrayal of such a peculiar spatiality. In the text, the "non-space" is depicted only negatively as a dark outside, and it emerges as the alternative site to a strictly hierarchical space of power. In his filmic transformation, *El hombre de la esquina rosada* [1961], director Miguel Picazo underscores the individual's creative production of space as opposed to a passive drifting. As an auditory cue, a voice off screen—unfathomable as space itself—recites several Borges poems that comment on the dissolution of fixed space.

Borges's famous short story "Tema del traidor y del héroe" ("Theme of the Traitor and the Hero") [1944] and Bernardo Bertolucci's *Strategia del ragno* (*A Spider's Stratagem*) [1970], the textual-filmic couple I study in my second chapter, both operate with multi-layered spaces and juxtapositions of sites from different temporal contexts. Similar to an Escher painting, the works blur the notions of foreground and background narrative and play with spatial emulations and repetitions of images and scenes. Thus, the text and the film illustrate a collapse of spatial certainties and the bewildering possibilities of a third space that emerges through a constant modification of perspectives.

Julio Cortázar's short story "Cartas de mamá" ("Letters from Mama") [1959] has been adapted twice, first by Manuel Antin (*La cifra impar*, The Odd Number) [1962], and second by Miguel Picazo (*Cartas de mamá*) [1979]. While Cortázar uses changing perspectives and the technique of indirect free speech to allude to spatial interchangeability and vagueness, Antin's film renders the topic through the interlocking of shots that belong to different spatio-temporal frames as well as the insertion of voices off screen that accompany the characters in locations that are dissociated from the speech contexts. Picazo emphasizes the yearning for a home or dwelling via lonely gazes through windows and cracks of doors. All three works break up a spatio-chronological narration and supplant it with atmospheric settings of recurring presences that are swallowed in an unbridgeable interstice time and again.

Juan Rulfo's *Pedro Páramo* (1955) is probably one of the most difficult Spanish American narrative texts to be adapted to a visual medium. Two directors have faced up to the challenge of showing a desolate village that is haunted by whispers and echoes in the dark: Carlos Velo, with *Pedro Páramo* [1966] and José Bolaños, with *Pedro Páramo—El hombre de la Media Luna* (Pedro Páramo, the Man of the Media Luna) [1976]. In Rulfo's novella, space is circumscribed through reverberations of bodiless echoes and reflections from invisible spatial boundaries. Comala is the resonating chamber for a fleeting chorus of voices of the dead. Both directors translate this radical *atopos* through the characters' encounter with an uncanny space, when they are recurrently confronted with highly similar, possibly identical, settings. Both Velo and Bolaños also experiment with auditory devices. Certain musical motifs are repeated in changing volumes, alluding to a character's spatial disquiet and feeling of vertigo, and to the overarching power of a space that annihilates its inhabitants.

In my last chapter, I analyze the illustrations of a "non-space" in Gabriel García Márquez's short story "La increíble historia de la cándida Eréndira y de su abuela desalmada" ("The Incredible and Sad Tale of Innocent Eréndira and Her Heartless Grandmother") [1972] and Ruy Guerra's film *Eréndira* [1982]. In this narration, the young prostitute Eréndira and her grandmother, who acts as her procuress, are traveling through a limitless desert. The themes of loneliness and exploitation, key concepts in many of García Márquez's texts, are expressed through space itself. The grandmother's obsessive accumulation of commodities in their tent in the desert is intended to fight her sense of a *horror vacui*. Yet, this accumulation process only entrenches her solitude and highlights the intrusive power of the spatial expanse surrounding the tent's inhabitants. In juxtaposition to her grandmother, the short story and the film show Eréndira's turning away from the crammed treasure chamber toward the desert, thus pointing to an alternative attunement to the spatial expanse on the lines of an "amor vacui." While García Márquez plays with these opposite cultural propensities toward space and belonging, the ending of Guerra's film, with its modification of the dialogues and long tracking shots of Eréndira's vanishing into the void, proposes a concept of radical openness.

As a comparative study of textual and cinematic instantiations of "non-spaces," this analysis highlights the potentials of inter-arts dialogues. Literary scholars have emphasized the written medium's power to convey settings beyond everyday experience. The selected Spanish American short texts aptly present elusive third spaces and their profound effects on people's relation to the world. The same can be said of film. Thanks to its pluri-medial nature, film may not only visualize the *atopos* in creative ways that are intrinsic to the medium; what is more, through the cinematic translations, the textual presentations of space develop further, and can now be read along with their spatial versions from the films in mind.

Building on Mikhail Bakhtin's thesis that a culture only reveals itself fully and profoundly in the eyes of another culture, Robert Stam proposes to extend this insight to the study of different media. According to Stam, "adaptation is potentially a way of one medium seeing another through a process of mutual illumination [and] of reciprocal relativization" (*Literature through Film: Realism, Magic, and the Art of Adaptation* 364–65). In line with this vision, I hope to provide compelling examples of such inter-arts cross-fertilizations between text and film.

Acknowledgments

Many people have helped me in the process of writing this book, which had its beginning as a dissertation in Spanish at the University of Virginia. I thank my thesis advisor, Gustavo Pellón, for his unwavering support and critical passion for my project, from its first draft up to its present form. The dialogues with him, together with his notes on the margins of the pages (peacock blue!) helped me find my way through many textual and linguistic mazes and taught me not to be afraid to make detours to encounter stimulating challenges. I am indebted to Randolph Pope for his initial guidance toward my topic and incisive criticism on the theoretical framework of my study. Many thanks to María Inés Lagos for her bibliographical suggestions on Spanish American cinema, and detailed feedback on several chapters of this text. At the University at Albany, SUNY, my thanks go to my colleagues in the Department of Languages, Literatures, and Cultures, especially Eloise Brière, Mary Beth Winn, and Maurice Westmoreland for their critical readings and inspiration, and to my graduate students for their intellectual curiosity during long seminar hours on Spanish American literature and film. Thanks to the anonymous readers for the Purdue Studies in Romance Literatures series for their suggestions, and to the production editor, Susan Y. Clawson, for sharing her practical wisdom with me; her many perceptive comments helped make my writing about sites of disquiet a material reality.

I am grateful to the Department of Spanish, Italian, and Portuguese at the University of Virginia for generously providing me a Dissertation Year Fellowship and to the Latin American Studies Program for granting me a fellowship to participate in the Summer Studies Program "Literatura argentina, crítica y creación" in Chaco, Argentina. Thanks to the State of New York/United University Professions Labor Management Committees at the University at Albany for awarding me an Individual Development Research Grant. All this enabled me to not get lost behind my desk writing about spaces in art, but to literally travel through spaces to gather material and alternate points of view.

Many thanks to Manuel Antin at the Argentinean Film University in Buenos Aires, who kindly shared with me his films and the unpublished correspondence with Julio Cortázar, and *gracias mil* to Karina Polesel for her persistence in helping me find information in the sometimes vaguely disquieting *porteño* research institutes. I am grateful to the crew at Alderman Library and the Robertson Media Center at the University of Virginia, to the staff at the Interactive Media Center at the University at Albany, the librarians in the German Film Museum and the Ibero-American Institute in Berlin (thanks to Ilja Elle, Anna and Duy Pham, my generous hosts), and to the staff at the library of Romance Studies at the University of Basel. A special thank you goes to Jesús Alonso-Regalado, the research librarian in Hispanic studies at the University at Albany, our one-of-a-kind detective of texts and films from all across the Americas.

An earlier version of Chapter 2 has appeared as "Space as a Metafictional Marker: Borges' 'Tema del traidor y del héroe' and Bertolucci's *Strategia del ragno*" in the *Bulletin of Hispanic Studies* 87.8 (2010): 977–94. I thank the journal editors for granting copyright permission. I also thank the M.C. Escher Company for permission to include a copy of Escher's *Print Gallery.*

I was fortunate to have had many sharp-eyed guides through languages that were not my own. Thanks to Cristina Ciudin and Danielle Carlotti-Smith for proofreading the quotes in French and Portuguese and to Neal McTighe for his revisions of the Italian quotes. My English and my thinking would both have remained clumsy without the attentiveness of Ilja Elle, Aalok Khandekar, Mark Prandolini, Joanna Springer, and particularly Girish Ratanpal.

There are no words—truly no words—to express my thanks to my parents and Mumi for their encouragement and love. And there are never enough words to thank all my friends and colleagues who challenged my positions in the most constructive ways and helped me conceptualize, think, phrase, discuss, persevere, and last but not least enjoy the act of writing.

Introduction

Spotting the Non-Space

Thinking Space: A First Approach

Space is a changing construct. It is created, experienced, and remembered individually and through social exchange and interaction with objects. Henri Lefebvre, one of the pioneers of the "spatial turn" in critical thinking, rejects any definition of a neutral space independent of the human perception. In *La production de l'espace*, he states:

> l'illusion de l'espace transparent, "pur" et neutre ne se dissipe que lentement. … L'espace ne peut plus se considérer comme une "essence," un objet distinct pour et devant les sujets, relevant d'une logique autonome… Il ne peut pas davantage se considérer comme une résultante et un résultat… Médium? Milieu? Intermédiaire? Oui, mais de plus en plus actif. (337, 472)

Many authors of recent studies on the perception of geographical, social, and political space go even further and argue that it is in the mind where space is created. James Corner describes both reality and space to be purely "constituted, or 'formed,' through our participation with things" (223). Homi K. Bhabha (in *Nation and Narration*) highlights the political space as a mental construct: "Nations, like narratives… only fully realize their horizons in the mind's eye" (1). From a different vantage point, Paul Virilio deconstructs the notion of a firm and passive outside space. The anthropologist diagnoses a political and ontological insecurity of space as being the result of the discoveries (explorations of space) and experiences and traumata of the twentieth and the beginning of the twenty-first centuries (the World Wars, the impact of the nuclear bombs of Hiroshima and Nagasaki, and terrorism). For

Virilio, the traditional denomination of space gave way to the concepts of movement, velocity, and of a relational vector. In this changed environment, people become passengers, perpetually on the move, in equally moved surroundings. Space, for the anthropologist, is as much an elaboration of reality as film. Virilio describes a passenger in a train, looking out of the window and seeing a moving landscape, similar to a projected landscape in a movie theater:

> La géographie variable du pays de la vitesse surgit dans l'histoire au siècle dernier. … L'ordre rural, la sérénité des champs, [sont] bouleversés par la révolution industrielle. … L'unidirectionnalité et l'uniformité se confondent avec la conquête du nouveau et dernier continent, celui de la vitesse. … Tout le mouvement de la physique moderne est esquissé ici [dans l'image d'un train mouvant le paysage] pour aboutir en 1916 à la théorie de la relativité généralisée, la désintégration du milieu. … Si la lucarne du train est bien une lanterne magique, elle fait apparaître les ombres de la science. … La voiture est aussi une chambre noire où les éléments de notre habitat quotidien deviennent particules en mouvement… La circulation devient nausée, comme si le télescopage des significations prenait valeur gastrique. (*Essai sur l'insécurité du territoire* 256–57)

As a result of new discoveries in physics and cosmological studies, the notion of a fixed outside space has already been challenged.[1] Therefore, any space, described in art, is even more insecure, to paraphrase Virilio, since space is modeled with an understanding of its relational and unstable (expanding, shrinking, shifting, etc.) character. Like outside spaces, many sites described in art have become, to cite Lefebvre again, "de plus en plus actif[s]" (472).

Designing Space: On the Page and in the Mind

It takes both a set of abstract signs, the text, and an active mind, the reader's realization, to construct a mental space out of black letters on the page. One might imagine a common setting, for instance, a person sitting in a closed room. The imagined spaces that are derived from this skimpy enunciation would vary enormously if one could sketch the "mind-space" of every reader. Three authors describe a scene that could loosely be subordinated to this setting. With just a few more words, the imagined scene (person—seat—room) becomes much richer in its connotative potentials. The first example is as follows: "Estaba sentado en unas bolsas de portland endurecido, solo, y a mi lado había un azadón con el mango blanco de cal" (10). The second one is: "La verán sentada en un sofá... sentada en un sofá tapizado con paño de lana, útil para la superación de los fríos polares pero de uso irrealísimo en estos trópicos tristes... la verán esperar sudada, sudada y apelotonada en un sofá sudado y apelotonado..." (13). The third example is: "Lunes. A bordo vuelo LanChile 511, Boeing 767, tramo LIM/LAX, del vuelo SLC/LAX; asiento 6D; actualmente arriba del Océano Pacífico, a la altura del balneario de Máncora, Perú. Es cierto: aquí hay mucho más espacio. El asiento se reclina hasta alcanzar la horizontalidad" (43). The first passage stresses a figure's loneliness amidst tools in a hut. The hardened cement, a material that normally serves to build and create, alludes to uselessness. The dirty hoe possibly signals rest after hard work. The colors mentioned are cheerless and dusky. The second figure has a much more comfortable seat. In the readers' mental space, this scene may appear in brighter light, due to the allusions to the tropical heat and a larger degree of comfort. The sofa captures the audience's attention; its material clearly does not fit into the environment. Furthermore, it reflects the character's emotion, since they are both described with the same adjectives. The woman is not neutrally sitting, but is "apelotonada." This participle may alter the reader's inner design of the scene. Did she hurry to the sofa? Did somebody else make her sit? Is she exhausted, impatient, or not at ease? The scene is not simply described to take place somewhere in the tropics, but "en estos trópicos tristes." For readers of French structuralist anthropology, the term echoes the book title by Claude Lévi-Strauss. These readers might add an element of irony to their mental visualization. Others may "paint" their interior vision with an individually chosen, melancholic tone. The third description remits to a formalist surrounding. Provided with technical data and a concise geographical reference, it refers to the neutral, air-conditioned environment of an airplane. When mentally designing their individual scene, the readers of this paragraph might be guided by personal experiences on board an aircraft; or they may think about films or pictures, or about a comfortable armchair for relaxing. They probably add further elements, such as colors, smells, and emotions from their personal experiences to elaborate their mental space, as it is evoked in the text. The settings for these spaces are quotes from Juan Carlos Onetti's *El pozo* (*The Pit*) [1939], Luis Rafael Sánchez's *La guaracha del Macho Camacho* (*Macho Camacho's Beat*) [1976], and Alberto Fuguet's *Las películas de mi vida* (*The Movies of My Life*) [2003]. Through the selection of words and their combination in a special semantic unit, they strongly guide the readers in their designing of a mental setting. However, the final "staging" of the characters into a mental environment is done by the readers, according to their interpretation of the reading, as well as to extratextual factors such as the personal, social, and historical realities to which they belong.

In my study of space in the short stories and novellas, I will proceed in a twofold manner. First, I shall closely analyze the selection and combination of words and sentences of the descriptions on the page. Second, I will approach the texts from a reception-oriented stance, and reflect on what this reading means, by seeking insight into the rhetorical and technical devices that are used in specific passages, to guide a reader in designing a mental space. I am aware of the balancing act between a close reading with its focus on the text itself[2] and a reader-oriented approach, shifting the main impetus to the receiver. The close reading is a useful tool for a detailed analysis and comparison of the distinctive, technical features of the two media. The approach that has been referred to as *reader-response* provides insight into individual, mental concretizations (in the sense that Wolfgang Iser used this term[3]) and to distinctive ways of interpretation.[4] It is of special importance with regard to the topic of space I analyze: The presentations of the places in the short stories and novellas I shall study require constantly active readers. We are confronted with vague spatial allusions or with disruptive and defamiliarizing sites. These settings bewilder, since they do not match any known category of literary spaces. As a result of their strangeness, they can become sources of imagination and lead the readers to design new spaces.

In *Utopian Audiences: How Readers Locate Nowhere,* Kenneth M. Roemer discusses the challenge of these texts for readers, and presents a wide spectrum of critical analyses of readers' reactions to the depiction of "unusual" places in literature. Although I do not entirely agree with Roemer's definition of the notions of *utopia* and *dystopia* (I will introduce the third notion of *atopos*), I agree with the potential of any "defamiliarizing" spatial description (be it *u-*, *dys-*, or *atopian*):

> During the past three decades there has been some shift toward emphasizing the disruptive functions and, thus, an enhancement of the reader's status… Lee Cullen Khanna and Gary Saul Morson speak of varieties of "defamiliarization"; Darko Suvin favors "cognitive estrangement" that can lead to the development of new perceptual skills; Jean Pfaelzer modifies this and uses "cognitive dissonance"… Peter Fitting and Phillip Wegner stress how utopias can "open up" spaces for conceptualization, and in the perhaps best-known articulation, Fredric Jameson claims that the literary utopia's function "is to provoke a fruitful bewilderment." (63)

Fredric Jameson, in his article "Of Islands and Trenches: Neutralization and the Production of Utopian Discourse," maintains that one of the main functions of utopian literature—and I would add, of any literature that contains descriptions of strange and defamiliarizing settings—is to challenge the readers' spatial perception. An utopian text forces its readers to think figuratively, to erect and "fill [an] empty space" (3). Jameson highlights the importance of active, co-creative readers and proposes to "understand the utopian text as a determinate text of *praxis* rather than a specific code of representation, a praxis which has less to do with the construction and perfection of someone's 'idea' of a 'perfect society' than it does with a concrete set of mental operations to be performed" (6). The spatial descriptions in the short narratives that I have chosen, precisely because they are strange, uncanny, and lack a concise spatial definition, might provoke such an "opening" and "broadening" of the readers' mental designs of space.

Presenting Space: From the Page to the Screen

A literary text is made out of a sequence of dark, abstract signs, separated by white spaces that have to be read according to certain conventions. We have to be able to see, to know the code, and finally to take the time to read through the text, before we can mentally set a stage, following the suggestions of, for instance, Onetti, Sánchez, or Fuguet. William H. Gass, in his essay "A True Lie-Minded Man," meditates on the abstract medium of writing, and verbalizes its potential:

> Like the mathematician, like the philosopher, the novelist makes things out of concepts. … The painter squeezes space

> through his pigments. Paint stains the fingers; the sculptor's hair is white with dust, but concepts have no physical properties; they do not permit smell or reflect light; they do not fill space or contain it, they do not age. "Five" is not wider, older or fatter than "four," "apple" isn't sweeter than "quince," rounder than "pear," smoother than "peach."… Sculptures take up space and gather dust. Concepts do not. They take us up. They invade us as we read, and they achieve, as our resistance and their forces vary, every conceivable degree of occupation. (262–63, 266)

Words are bodiless. They do not pretend to represent mimetically any object or to fuse with their signified. While a reader is free to project an idealized image of a scene beyond the structure of the text, visual media often present spaces in the two-dimensional reduction.[5] Paintings may disrupt this peculiar, traditional two-dimensionality via special technical devices. Cy Twombly's or Jackson Pollock's huge paintings of thick layers of splattered colors or their cut-through canvases show this transgressional impetus. A film, on the contrary, cannot transgress its two-dimensional projection of a three-dimensional space. It has to present a setting as soon as it shows a performance. A stage director of a play or a film necessarily has to show a "spatial effect" (to paraphrase Barthes's notion of a "reality effect") of a preceding place, in order to convey the idea of the figures' movements within three-dimensionality.

Seymour Chatman, in *Story and Discourse—Narrative Structure in Fiction and Film,* distinguishes between five main technical features of the cinematic media that communicate the idea of a three-dimensional space: First, the simple size of an object structures its environment. Chatman gives the example of a "two-inch lizard shot close up [which] will glower like a dinosaur on the screen when superimposed, by back-projection, against Tokyo skyscrapers" (97). This example also contains another device that conveys the idea of a depth of field, not mentioned by the critic, which is the technique of superimposition. By positioning an object in front of another, the idea of three-dimensionality can be conveyed. Second, Chatman mentions the shadow of an object, as an element referring to the composition's spatial dimension. The third device he refers to is the position of an object within the frame of the camera, and in relation to other objects in the setting. Fourth comes the lighting of an object, including the degree, the kind, and the color of the focusing light. The last parameter Chatman mentions is the degree of clarity. If an object is in focus, the human eye interprets it to be closer to the lens. An object shown out of focus or through a distorting lens is seen to be more distant. Ira Koenigsberg, in his essay "The Art of Technology: Contours of Space in the Science Fiction Film," mentions two more features: the linear perspective based on orthographic projection and, as a necessary pre-condition, the assumption of "a single centralized viewer" (*Space and Beyond* 67).[6]

In comparison to other visual arts, the main characteristic of cinema is movement. Generally, the images unroll in such a quick succession that the human eye is unable to perceive the cuttings between the particular shots. This film apparently unfolds instantaneously, in the here and now of the cinema show (Paech 185). However, as Gilles Deleuze in *Cinéma 2: L'image-temps* reminds us, the image on-screen is necessarily an image of a past presence (355). In its beginnings, in the last decade of the nineteenth century, film was close to theater. Instead of a presentation onstage, cinema showed a previously recorded projection through the fixed apparatus, with the advantage of repeatability without exhausting the actors. The Lumière brothers' first films are captured through a fixed camera, with a single shot. Such a position of the camera is similar to the position of a spectator in the audience of a theater, with a fixed point of view (Paech 5–8). Since then, over the intervening century, film distanced itself from theater. Increasingly, the camera became mobile and projected multifaceted montages of shots, counter-shots, flashbacks, or flash forwards, ellipses, jump cuts, cross-fading images, dimming, and many more.

Compared to a painting, and to a lesser degree, to a play performance, film conditions the viewer's eye much more rigorously. Walter Benjamin, in his seminal essay "The Work of Art in the Age of Mechanical Reproduction," highlights the impact of what he calls the medium's "shock effect" on the spectators. As a result of the preselection of the frames, perspectives, and the sudden changes of images, the observer's gaze cannot linger on certain details of a filmic image, but is "assailed" by the change of place and focus. Film's distracting element is based

> on changes of place and focus which periodically assail the spectator. Let us compare the screen on which a film unfolds with the canvas of a painting. The painting invites the spectator to contemplation; before it the spectator can abandon himself to his associations. Before the movie frame he cannot do so. No

> sooner has his eye grasped a scene than it is already changed. ... The spectator's process of association in view of these images is indeed interrupted by their constant, sudden change. This constitutes the shock effect of the film, which, like all shocks, should be cushioned by heightened presence of mind. (240)

The lens presents a set and displays it from a certain angle. It is capable of changing its position with regard to a filmed object. A camera might zoom in or zoom out, swing around a character or proceed in a parallel movement to a moved figure (Paech 122–29).

During the showing of a film, the passively sitting viewers seem to be released from their own physical and spatial realities. Together with the characters, they pass through walls, fly to the stars, or descend to the center of the earth; they see the world upside down, zoom in and travel in a submarine through the veins and arteries of a human body, climb the peak of a mountain without using an oxygen mask, or are vertiginously catapulted to space-times they never experience in everyday life. Space, in this medium of moved characters, evoked by an equally moved camera, is often presented as a fixed environment, an explicit and stable background for the figures.

Other films—among them, those I will analyze—highlight an immanently different space that is not fixed, but altering. Benjamin, in the essay mentioned above, draws attention to the technical potential of the cinematic medium to present sites in such a way that they challenge our common perception of space:

> With the close-up, space expands; with slow motion, movement is extended. The enlargement of a snap-shot does not simply render more precise what in any case was visible, though unclear: it reveals entirely new structural formations of the subject. So, too, slow motion not only presents familiar qualities of movement but reveals in them entirely unknown ones. ... Evidently a different nature opens itself to the camera than opens to the naked eye. ... The camera introduces us to unconscious optics as does psychoanalysis to unconscious impulses. (*Illuminations* 238–39)

The cinematic medium mechanically repeats, enlarges, minimizes, cuts, or stitches together various shots, montages, and images, and thus offers alternative techniques to present new spatial configurations beyond our perception of "real" outside space.

Film is a "hybrid art" (Paech 166), capable of embracing and integrating other artistic expressions, and therefore, of including different ways of creating space within its own presentation. The screen might, for instance, show a written text, and transform the audience into a reading public, which allows for the inclusion of individual spatial projections. With regard to the presentation of space, the technical development of sound is of particular importance. Unlike abstract signs on a page, sound waves transcend space. They do not lose dimension when they are recorded. Surpassing spatial boundaries, they are "present" during the film screening, in contrast to the projected objects on the screen. Robert Stam, in *Film Theory: An Introduction,* remarks:

> The reproduction of sound, unlike the reproduction of the three-dimensional visual phenomena, involves no dimensional loss—both original and copy involve mechanical radiant energy transmitted by pressure waves in the air; thus we perceive sound as three-dimensional. ... Sound goes around corners, while light rays are blocked. Since sound penetrates and pervades space, it molds a heightened sense of presence. (214)

A film, despite being a manifestation of an irretrievable past presence, partly recovers the claims of being an art of presence, due to the sound track. Music, spoken words, and ambient noise are obviously not creating a space, but they are able to pervade and therefore to connect the space of the audience with the projection to a much higher degree than the apparent realistic presentation of spaces on the wall of a dark room. In the films I will analyze in the following pages, sound becomes a main device to fathom the adverse and slippery spaces.

The Concept of *Atopos*: A Clarification

The conceptual opposition of *topos* (locus, place, room, space, spot) and *utopos* has a long tradition. The *topos* refers to a real geographical place, measurable and accessible in its extension. The *utopos*, in contrast, points toward a precisely unreal, projected locus beyond human experience, be it the expression of a religious, political, social or philosophical ideal state. Its depiction may vary from a purely imaginary tale, intended for pleasure or entertainment, or a rigorous moral treatise meant to edify or convince. In the *Republic*, one of the first texts on utopia, Plato maps out an ideal and just social environment for the polis.[7] Saint Augustine, in *City of God*, outlines the paradisiacal state of a God-made city, according to the Christian belief and practice, in contrast to an earthly city, symbolized by Babylon. Thomas More, in 1516, with the book that coins the name of the genre, writes a sharp commentary on the social and political life of sixteenth-century England, but he also creates an artifact of, and contribution to, this same history. His imagined Utopia is an island, described by the fictitious Portuguese traveler Raphael Hythloday, who has sailed with Amerigo Vespucci on his last three voyages to the American continent. In the words of the narrating figure, Utopia is a space of marvelous economic, political, and sexual equality, of welfare and peacefulness: "But this thing I believe verily… that there is in no place of the world neither a more excellent people neither a more flourishing commonwealth" (164). This nowhere-space has positive connotations. As David Harris Sacks, in his introduction to More's novel, remarks: "The name *Utopia* is a compound Greek word meaning literally 'no place' or 'nowhere.' But… in the brief poem 'Of Utopia' [sung by the bard of the island] the name is made to pun on the Greek word *eutopia*, which means 'happy' or 'fortunate place'" (15). The favorable connotation of utopia as not only a different, but also a better world has marked utopian literature throughout the centuries (Tower Sargent 558). Utopia's opposite is the equally projected negative utopia or *dystopia*, an imaginary place where people lead dehumanized and fearful lives. Like their positive counterparts, the negative utopias, such as in Aldous Huxley's *Brave New World* [1932], George Orwell's *1984* [1949], and many science fiction films, such as *Alphaville* [1965], *Blade Runner* [1982], or *Dark City* [1998], are projected places of nowhere. Both *dystopia* and *utopia* are never naïve or out of touch with the real world. On the contrary, their depiction serves as a means of understanding a present social or political situation, be it via the reference to a nonexistent good place or its reverse, a site where all possible terrors are carried to extremes.

Approaching the short stories and novellas that are the primary sources for this analysis, I encounter designs of spaces that are not *topic, utopic* or *dystopic.* A simple street corner, painted pink, a town with a staged performance (Borges), spaces of absence, longing, and guilt (Cortázar's "Cartas de mamá"), a haunted plain of blistering heat, invaded by bodiless whispers (Rulfo's *Pedro Páramo*), a wasteland, afflicted by a "wind of disgrace" (García Márquez's *Eréndira*)—all these places cannot be subsumed entirely under one of the previously discussed spatial conceptions. They are too vague to be *topoi*. Likewise, they are not clearly projected, non-existent *utopias* or *dystopias*. I also do not consider them to be mere symbolic spaces, concrete entities that refer to abstract elements, psychic drives, or experiences. The spaces designed in the short narratives are much more ambiguous and potentially active. They are disquieting; this is perhaps the adjective that characterizes all of them best. A character within such an unpredictable space feels estranged, sometimes frightened, and never at ease. These adverse spaces possess a negative quality: they allude to common spatial characteristics, and at the same time, paradoxically, negate them.

A third term, less known and much less defined, may reflect the literary evocations and experience of space in a more precise way: the *atopos*. *Webster's New International Dictionary* briefly defines *atopy* as "out of the way" or "unusual," and the adjective *atopic* as "not in the usual place" (139). Michel Foucault, in his lecture "Des espaces autres," introduces yet another notion—the *heterotopos*—which has certain commonalities with the concept of the *atopos* I will elaborate. He defines it as a real space, where different places are juxtaposed: "L'hétérotopie a le pouvoir de juxtaposer en un seul lieu réel plusieurs espaces" (758). For Foucault, the paradigmatic *heterotopos* is the ship, a movable space, which at the same time, lacks spatial characteristics: "Le bateau, c'est un morceau flottant d'espace, un lieu sans lieu, qui vit par lui-même, qui est fermé sur soi, et qui est livré en même temps à l'infini de la mer" (*Dits et écrits* 762). His outline, however, remains rather tentative and mostly focused on the characteristic of a plurality of spaces within one space. In contrast to the *heterotopos*, the term and concept of *atopos* has received more thorough explanations, which highlight commonalities with the spaces encountered in the literary works under consideration. Rich in potential but vague in its definition, the *atopos* has been a central notion in three theoretical studies. Although the approaches and procedures are distinct from each other, and also from my own, they highlight a common feature of the alternative space, which is useful for my study. Roland Barthes, in *Fragments d'un discours amoureux* [1977], Michel de Certeau, in *L'invention du quotidien—I. Arts de faire* [1980], and Marc Augé, in *Non-lieux: Introduction à une anthropologie de la surmodernité* [1992], propose concepts that share the common element of a real, active space, which eludes being defined. It therefore elaborates on two of the main characteristics of the spaces in the *nueva narrativa* fictions.

In his poetic, sensuously written analysis of the rhetoric of love, Barthes defines the *atopos* as the slippery, non-classifiable, ceaselessly unforeseen originality of the beloved other: "L'atopie résiste à la description, à la définition, au langage… Atopique, l'autre fait trembler le langage: on ne peut parler *de* lui, *sur* lui; tout attribut est faux, douloureux, gaffeur, gênant: l'autre est *inqualifiable* (ce serait le vrai sens d'*atopos*)" (44). According to this outline, the lover is the radical and inconceivable other. And it is this characteristic that makes the committed subject love this impregnable "you," and thus, to pursue Barthes's argument, makes their mutual (and mute) love original. Barthes highlights two reasons for the difficulties in defining their love: first, the emotional closeness of the loving subject to the beloved, and second, the incapacity of the linguistic code to capture the experience. Any definition of love brings the emotion to an end.

Michel de Certeau, philosopher, theologian, friar, historian, and professor of medieval and Renaissance literature, chair of the Department of Historic Anthropology of Belief Systems at the Parisian École des Hautes Études en Sciences Sociales, develops his notion of a *non-lieu*. In the first part of *L'invention du quotidien—I. Arts de faire*, de Certeau analyzes a section of Daniel Defoe's *Robinson Crusoe,* when the famous literary character discovers a footprint in the sand of his island. The margins of Robinson's self-proclaimed territory have been marked, literally imprinted by an absent force. The frontiers are blurred and challenged, not by a present invader, but by an absent ghostlike figure (it is not until later that Robinson will meet and name the intruder, Friday):

> Robinson Crusoé indiquait déjà lui-même comment une faille s'introduisit dans son empire scripturaire. Pendant un temps, son entreprise est… interrompue, et hantée, par un absent qui revient sur les bords de l'île. … Instabilité du bornage: la frontière cède à de l'étranger. Sur les marges de la page, la trace d'un invisible fantôme (an apparition) [*sic*] trouble l'ordre. … Le territoire de l'appropriation est altéré par la trace de quelque chose qui n'est pas là et n'a pas lieu. … Le roman de 1719 indique déjà le non-lieu (une trace, qui mord sur les bords). (226)

In de Certeau's *non-lieu*, a mere trace unhinges the fixed borderlines and spatial securities. Robinson initially intruded and invented (literally and also in the etymological sense of the Latin *inventio* stressing both the creative act and the intrusion) the space, but the island becomes "outlandish," and changes from a fixed place to a deferred "non-space" of doubt that lacks its former unit and reliability. The main trait of this *atopos* is its adversity to the figure that is situated within. Its changeableness and unpredictable movement—the place itself is violently devouring its borderlines—foreclose spatial domination and definition.

Twelve years later, Marc Augé publishes a meditation on late capitalist, Western, urban environments. Despite the fact that he is "spatially" close to Barthes and de Certeau, since he works in the same research center, his approach clearly differs from theirs. In his *Non-lieux: Introduction à une anthropologie de la surmodernité*, Augé introduces the notion of "supermodernity" to describe the logic of excessive space of circulation that lacks personal inscription and connection.[8] He calls these spaces "supermodern" or *non-lieux*, following the concept formation of Michel de Certeau. Examples of those are airports, trains, numbered hotel rooms, malls that are similar to each other, corridors of metro stations that allow people and goods to enter and to circulate without establishing individual relationships to their surroundings. Taking their toll, they oblige the users to possess and exhibit certain special features, to show approval IDs, boarding passes, and to declare the weight of their belongings. Augé notes that "d'une certaine manière, l'utilisateur du non-lieu est toujours tenu de prouver son innocence" (128). In exchange, these spaces promise a rapid delivery and transportation. Their aim is to make users and objects pass through and leave the space as quickly as possible. The materials that prevail in those formalistic areas are translucent or reflecting, and all man-made (glass, metal, mirrors). The users' views are either directed toward an aim (a customs clearance behind glass barriers, a terminal that has been announced beforehand), or are reflected on themselves, as they walk along the metallic barriers or mirrors alongside the restaurants and duty-free shops.

Non-lieux allow no individual inscription. The users, directed by signs, scarcely communicate with other individuals, but instead with machines: "Les non-lieux réels de la surmodernité… ont ceci de particulier qu'ils se définissent aussi par les mots ou les textes qu'ils nous proposent: leur mode d'emploi en somme, qui s'exprime selon le cas de façon prescriptive… , prohibitive… ou informative. [Ce sont] des espaces où les individus sont censés d'interagir qu'avec des textes" (120–21). The anthropologist contrasts this self-contained, anonymous "supermodern" space with three distinct spaces: the poetic Baudelairean modern space, re-evoked by Walter Benjamin in his Parisian *Passages*, where old and new are interwoven and interpreted inter-dependently. Secondly, Augé posits these *non-spaces* of the daily (rites of) passage "par opposition à la notion sociologique de lieu, associée par Mauss et toute une tradition ethnologique à celle de culture localisée dans le temps et l'espace" (48). Traditional anthropologic space is meant to be identifying, relational, and historic, in order to produce a sense of spatial belonging.[9] Thirdly, Augé asserts: "le non-lieu est le contraire de l'utopie: il existe et il n'abrite aucune société organique" (140). Again, the *non-place* is difficult to capture: in part, because it does not reveal itself to the subject (similar to Barthes's description of the beloved as the total other), but presents mere reflecting facades and repetitive room layouts. An additional difficulty to seize it is the result of the subject's position. Far from being a distant observer with a privileged, elevated perspective, such as the *flâneur* in Baudelaire's *Tableaux parisiens* (*Parisian Scenes*) [1861], languorously gazing over Paris out of the window in his garret at Montmartre, or the narrator of Poe's short story, sitting behind the window of the café in London, when spotting the enigmatic "Man of the Crowd" [1840], the "users" in this different space, as in any architectonic unit, perceive themselves to be within its three-dimensionality. This last trait is comparable to the second difficulty outlined by Barthes, characteristic of the system of language, which is incapable of any true representation, but which cannot be avoided either. Barthes's, de Certeau's, and Augé's elaborations of the "non-space" testify to the concept's intrinsic resistance to definition—definition in the triple sense of, first, an explanation of a term, second, a spatial demarcation, and third, a finalizing closure.

The settings of the short stories and novellas I will study are not all formalist spaces of late capitalism, as described by Augé. However, they are comparable to those sites in their slipperiness. For instance, characters feel queasy in the adverse, incommunicable environment of, for instance, an immense wasteland (Rulfo's *Pedro Páramo*), at a site of mirrors (Borges's "Tema del traidor y del héroe"), or at places of inner loneliness (Cortázar's "Cartas de mamá"). These spaces of displacement, deferral, and absence are manifesting themselves in the traces of a past or a longed for presence or in the echoes that reverberate from invisible walls. The meager characterizations of the concepts parallel the spaces encountered in the short stories and novellas—the *atopos* is a tentative and often indirect circumscription and has no fixed delineation. (In the following, I will mostly use the denomination of *atopos* to describe the alternative "non-spaces," given its previous critical elaborations. From an etymological point of view, the terms of *ectopos* ("out, out of, or off place") or *allotopos* ("different, other place") also capture the characteristics of the spaces under consideration.[10]

The sensation of readers and critics, facing such a blurry definition, may reflect the characters' perception of their environment within the fictitious works. Like them, we do not feel at ease on such moving terminological ground, only tangible via a negative approach. Yet, the paradoxical place, which is described as indescribable, is not a new feature of the texts chosen for this study. In the Judeo-Christian tradition, the *atopos* has a famous predecessor, another place on earth (therefore not utopian), which also radically differs from earthly bondage, and which posed many challenges to being defined throughout the centuries: the Garden of Eden. Alessandro Scafi, in his essay "Mapping Eden: Cartographies of the Earthly Paradise," describes the space beyond spatial conventions, evoked in a text. Referring to the problem of cartography of the biblical Garden, Scafi remarks:

> A space which had to be shown on maps as finite and limited was in fact a world in itself, a boundless universe paradoxically encapsulated and bounded within a sensible space. In such a context, mapping the location of Paradise, and charting its ontologically different time and space on a world map, presents a fascinating cartographic paradox: mapping a place on earth but not of earth. (56)

The biblical Eden, similar to the enigmatic Borgesian South, Rulfo's Comala, or García Márquez's desert, all lack current spatial conventions. But despite—or maybe because of—their elusiveness, the sites have been the source of manifold artistic re-elaborations, be they literary, musical, or visual. The visual presentations of these other spaces require the artists, readers, and viewers to literally "set" a scene by transforming a paradoxical, imagined site without spatial finitude and boundaries into a fixed space, for instance, on a map, onto a copper engraving, in a picture, or on the celluloid strip of a film.

Excursus: *Atopos* and Solitude

Barthes, de Certeau, and Augé not only design similar spaces to the ones I encounter in the literary texts; they also refer to an effect of the conceptualized *atopos* upon its occupants. This effect is also to be found in the selected short stories and novellas: the deep feeling of estrangement and solitude in the characters.[11] In Barthes's conception, man's isolation originates from the intrinsic slipperiness and failure of language to capture and adequately present concepts and thoughts. The lover is lonely due to his or her incapacity to define the beloved and to communicate with him or her. The beloved does not liberate the loving subject from inner reclusion; instead, both remain in "otherness." De Certeau evokes a lonesome Robinson, who rules a space, before he dominates and names the other human being in his self-proclaimed kingdom. The two characters on the secluded island are never equal. The passengers of Augé's urban *non-lieux* share the space with many others. All similar to each other in their "use" of the place, they nevertheless remain alone. The individuals in Augé's design are no languorous strollers or avid observers, seduced by sudden charming views. They all hurry to leave the formalist "non-space" as quickly as possible. Any attempt to establish communication, be it only a brief eye-contact, is difficult, as the gazes are directed toward a clear aim: "C'est à de tels déplacements du regard, à de tels jeux d'images… que peuvent conduire, à mon sens… les manifestations les plus caractéristiques de ce que j'ai proposé d'appeler 'surmodernité.' Celle-ci impose en effet aux consciences individuelles des expériences et des épreuves très nouvelles de solitude" (117). According to Augé, human beings undergo an intense isolation in the formal surroundings of late capitalism. The concluding sentence of his analysis, therefore, points toward a new field of investigation, the study of loneliness in the masses: "Il y aura donc place demain, il y a peut-être déjà place aujourd'hui, malgré la contradiction apparente des termes, pour une ethnologie de la solitude" (150).

The characters in the estranged settings in the literary works are also deeply lonely. Borges's heroes dance and fight with others, but in the end remain alone. Cortázar's character Luis from "Cartas de mamá" lives in a marriage full of guilt and neurotic lack of communication. Juan Preciado in Rulfo's *Pedro Páramo* strays through the ruins of Comala, temporarily guided by different figures that will all vanish. He dies in total isolation. In García Márquez's "La increíble y triste historia de la cándida Eréndira y de su abuela desalmada," the girl's lover, Ulises, is no liberating hero for her: after he has killed her oppressive grandmother, Eréndira leaves him without explaining herself. To varying degrees, all figures in the adverse surroundings suffer social exclusion and intimate isolation. Their most striking common experiences are a deep loneliness and disillusion with the communicative power of language. Some characters desperately try to overcome their solitude but fail. Others already have given up any hope of crossing the "prohibited territory" of separation, as we read in Cortázar's text. Others lose themselves in the mighty wind of disgrace, drifting beyond the horizon (Eréndira) or in the floating echo of the deserted streets of a town of death (*Pedro Páramo*). The protagonists in those stories and films, like the lover in Barthes's, the islanders in de Certeau's, and the passengers in Augé's studies, are radically isolated. Many fail to recognize the active power of the adverse "non-spaces," which are not only mirroring the characters' solitude, but also, to a large degree, creating it.

The Potentials and Limits of Inter-arts Translation

The notion of adaptation covers a vast semantic spectrum. It has been critically addressed in academia; readers and viewers have also discussed it in more emotive ways. Brian McFarlane, in *Novel to Film—An Introduction to the Theory of Adaptation*, describes the most common reactions to the practice. On the one end of the spectrum, he situates angry readers complaining about "novels as being 'betrayed' by boorish film-makers" (3). Avid moviegoers, on the other side, who refuse to read a single line of the adapted literary text, "regard the practice of comparing film and novel as a waste of time" (3). Although there are skeptics in both camps, the dissatisfied readers generally outnumber the dissatisfied viewers. The first reason for this imbalance might be the result of the medial conditions, as elaborated above. The readers, after creating their mental images of the world of a novel, when watching a film, are confronted with a setting of somebody else's fantasy. It is quite an effort to abandon one's own images and to engage with different versions, which, in addition, change according to an outside rhythm (the film spool unrolling mechanically). The second reason for many readers' frustration, when confronted with a cinematic adaptation, is of an ideological character. Despite many new artistic elaborations and brilliant critical analyses in media studies, Western cultural elites often still favor the older medium of literary production to cinema. However, poststructuralist thinkers, who highlight the plurality and inter-relation of discourses against a proclaimed medial hierarchy, have increasingly challenged such a discourse of origins. It has also been discussed by social scientists and critical theorists, who unmask the presumed dominance of high versus low culture, arguing that the "opposition high-low is intrinsic not to the object under scrutiny but to the assumptions we bring to these (or any) works. Thus, bringing the concerns of popular culture to bear on works of 'high' culture debunks the latter and undermines the opposition between them" (Bal, *Reading "Rembrandt": Beyond the Word-Image Opposition* 8). A common argument in the discussion on adaptation is the aspect of fidelity.[12] McFarlane highlights the limitations of the conception:

> Fidelity criticism depends on a notion of the text as having and rendering up to the (intelligent) reader a single, correct "meaning" which the film-maker has either adhered to or in some way violated and tampered with... The insistence on fidelity... tends to ignore the idea of adaptation as an example of convergence among the arts. (8–10)

By privileging the written text, such an approach hardly ever takes into account the specific technical characteristics and artistry in both media. The notions of origin and creative source lose ground, according to the idea of a text as a momentary enunciation within a network of preceding and future enunciations.

Mieke Bal convincingly describes any adaptation as an intertextual praxis. In her essay "Dispersing the Gaze: Focalization," she stresses that, "the 'translation' of a novel into a film is not a one-by-one transposition of a story element into an image, but a visual working-through of the novel's most important aspects and their meanings. ... All this is... [a matter] of intertextuality" (in

Looking In—The Art of Viewing 57–58). The notion of intertextuality entails a dispersal of origins and affirms a semantic opening, a (sometimes uncanny) plurality of meaning. A film can become a new source, or rather an additional knot within the woven texture of a broader intermedial discourse.

The relations between a preceding and a succeeding work are manifold. However allusive or explicit they are, in the light of poststructuralist thought, they are no longer defined to be based on notions of dependence and loyalty. The director of a film might search for an analogous mode of expression, design a critical response to a preceding text, or simply use a novel as a point of departure for his or her own artistic explorations (Michelangelo Antonioni's *Blow-Up* would be emblematic of a creative translation of Julio Cortázar's short story "Las babas del diablo"). According to Jorge Urrutia, in his semiotic analysis *Imago litterae: cine literatura*, "debe haber una diferencia, por mínima que esta sea. Adaptar es trasformar, cambiar, hacer un nuevo objeto. Otro objeto" (77–78). Urrutia underscores that not only is the "derived" work of art necessarily different from the one it is based on, but that it also alters the preceding one. Both works affect each other: "Si sólo es posible un nuevo texto, el primero, el *adaptado*, no será sino *adoptado*" (78; emphasis in original). From this perspective, cinematic adaptation is the result of a polyphonic and dialogic relationship between the equal value media text and film. I consider the concept of dialogue to be crucial, since it stresses the progressive character of the artistic relation, as well as medial equality. The later artists open up the dialogue on reinterpretation and on the production and proliferation of meaning(s).

The notions of intertextuality and dialogue used above bring to mind the theoretical framework proposed by Mikhail Bakhtin, such as *heteroglossia, chronotope*, and *dialogism*. Bakhtin's approach, although initially developed for the analysis of novels, has been fruitfully applied to the film genre. Among other critics, Eva Maria Stadler draws attention to film's dialogic relation to the textual medium, as well as the cinematographic medium's intrinsic "dialogism," due to the various technical devices and to film's potential to include other media: "Dialogic relations between the film and its pre-texts, between sound and image, between juxtaposed images as well as among various elements of the sound track can introduce multiple competing voices. Incorporated genres within the film can expand intertextual possibilities" (16). Film becomes a critical comment on a literary text or the point of departure for further artistic dialogues. The adaptations I will discuss in the following chapters venture into multiple inter-arts dialogues and explore new facets within this open concept of adaptation as translation and variation.

From Intertextuality to Intermediality

The word *intertextuality*, often used in critical studies on adaptation during the last fifty years, has a terminological flaw. Again, it stresses the primacy of the text. Yet the intertextual model, introduced by Julia Kristeva as a re-conceptualization of Bakhtin's concept of dialogism, challenges the traditional hegemony of the written word and defines the notion of a text very broadly.[13] According to Robert Stam "intertextual theory… sees the artist as dynamically orchestrating pre-existing texts and discourses. … [Intertextuality] does not limit itself to a single medium; it allows for dialogic relations with other arts and media, both popular and erudite" (*Film Theory: An Introduction* 203). But if the activity consists in investigating different media and highlighting the distinct medial conditions of the enunciations, the insistence on the notion of a text in the name is unprofitable. Instead of intertextuality, the denomination of intermediality proves to be more accurate. In the light of my study on both examples in literature and film, this term points toward the medial distinctions and processes of inter-medial translations in a more precise way.

The term *intermediality* has been used since the 1990s. Similar to the notion of intertextuality, the label comprises a wide range of definitions that may even contradict each other. I follow the concept as elaborated by a group of researchers at the German University of Konstanz, which has had a major impact on Western European studies on inter-arts relations.[14] Etymologically, the term *medium* derives from the Greek *meson*, defining an element between two distant objects, a common area or public way.[15] According to Joachim Paech, in "Artwork—Text—Medium: Steps en Route to Intermediality," a medium is no neutral deposit or mere means of transportation from a sender to a receiver. Similar to intertextuality, intermediality is built upon the Bakhtinian conception of dialogue.[16] In a more detailed explanation than

Marshall McLuhan, Paech underscores that any medium actively participates in the shaping of an artistic expression. He identifies a medium "functionally in a purpose (means), topologically at a place (middle), as a substitute, a body or apparatus, or a corporate and institution. ... [A medium] is not the particular appearance of that for which 'it' acts as a mediator" (6). The first two clarifications of a medium as a means and middle from a sender to a receiver are well established in the critical discourse; the third one might need further explication. In approaching a medium as a substitute, Paech starts out from a main obstacle in analyzing media: A medium by itself is necessarily invisible in the moment of the artistic enunciation.[17] Setting the examples of light and air as media of visual communication, Paech affirms that "nothing appears without air and light, but this only applies if air itself does not appear, for instance, in the form of fog, and light does not simply blind one's eye" (7). Light and air, because they are bodiless, make possible the presentation of a statement or message.

In this regard, the notion of a medium is comparable to the notion of the Derridean trace. In *La dissémination,* Jacques Derrida circumscribes the written word similarly to later medial theorists, when they refer to artistic media:

> Attentifs, fascinés, collés à *ce qui* se présente, nous ne pouvons voir sa *présence* même, elle ne se présente pas, ni la visibilité du visible, l'audibilité de l'audible, le milieu, l'"air" qui disparaît ainsi en laissant paraître. ... Toute la force d'écriture... c'est surtout le simulacre [...] d'une identité sans cesse disloquée, déplacée, renvoyée hors d'elle-même. (381, 394–95)

Paech comparatively asserts a medium's invisibility and constant deferral.[18] In order to represent a previous enunciation, in a delay in time and space, it has to be transparent. Through the representation in a new spatio-temporal frame, the medium stresses the difference between the two settings. Therefore, it functions as a substitute, perpetually oscillating between a former, irretrievable "here and now" and a present reference to a "there and then." Paech concludes that "media... are nothing other than 'translations' of transformations" (6). During the act of translating, media ideally transform an enunciation, without manifesting themselves. The notion of a medium outlined above, which defers and vanishes in the very moment of representation, leads to a conception of intermediality as a differential, oscillating praxis. In this line of thought, an intermedial study is the analysis of an artistic translation—in the literal and also in the etymological sense of a *translation*, as a "movement of carrying over, across or beyond, a shifting from one place to another, an act, process or instance" (2429) according to *Webster's International Dictionary*.

This concept of intermediality is crucial for my analysis, since it points toward the in-betweenness of the respective medial enunciations and highlights the progression and continuous oscillation between literature and cinema. It challenges and reverses the simple vector from a source (a literary text) to an end product (a film). Instead of focusing on the two extremes, it measures the space in between them. One of the earliest meditations on the change in reading and viewing habits, which goes along with the double experience of the literary and cinematic media, is Bertolt Brecht's note on the cinematic adaptation of his *Two-Penny Opera*: "The old forms of mediation do not remain unaltered by the newly emerging and do not persist neutrally next to them. The viewer of a film reads stories in a different manner. Likewise, the one who writes stories is himself a viewer of films" (256; my translation). While reading the short stories and novellas by Borges, Cortázar, Rulfo, and García Márquez, we are not exclusively "within" the literary works, since we know that they have been the bases for adaptations. Likewise, when watching Picazo's, Bertolucci's, Antin's, Bolaños's, Velo's, and Guerra's films, the previous texts do not entirely abandon us either. The viewing readers as well as the reading viewers are subject to the intermedial tensions outlined above.

The theoretical framing of intermediality stresses the presence of an enunciation in the oscillating disappearance of the representation and the opening up of the field of interpretation, which allows enriching changes of perspectives. The approach also takes into account the location of the recipient, the situation of the readers, and the viewers of a film, who find themselves in between the media. Besides this theoretical opening and the focus on the position of the viewer and reader, there is also a thematic reason to favor this intermedial approach. Many figures and narrators of the literary texts and films that I chose deal with the topic of the artistic medium itself. Media are discussed, scrutinized, and challenged intradiegetically in the short stories and films. The initial narrator in Borges's "Tema del traidor y del héroe," for example, meditates on the status of the text to be written. Juan Preciado, the protagonist in Velo's film *Pedro Páramo*, increasingly mistrusts his perception. Most of the texts and films show a self-reflexive (meta-narrative and meta-filmic) endeavor that encourages a medial investigation. Taking into account this common theme, the inter-medial approach might do justice to this interest in the works. It can reflect the investigations in the short narratives and films and mirror them in a critical investigation on and in-between them.

Chapter One

Into Spatial Vagueness

Jorge Luis Borges's and Miguel Picazo's *Hombre de la esquina rosada*

A major element in many of Borges's short fictions is the relationship between reality, human perception, and language. How do we make sense of the world around us and of ourselves within it? Is our language a reliable tool to communicate or is it a means of dispersion and misunderstanding? Borges's texts do not present single answers. Instead, they evoke puzzling worlds with doubtful protagonists who are uncertain whether they dream or are awake, or whether they are criminals, victims, or even the creators of the fictitious webs in which they live. Donald L. Shaw, in *Borges' Narrative Strategy*, compares the texts with "parables or fables which illustrate aspects of the general collapse of rational or religious certainties in our modern world, and the bewildering possibilities which thus emerge" (2). Containing an "implicit 'what if…?' [or] 'suppose that…'" (2), as Shaw describes it, the short stories expose dizzying, vertiginous, and fantastic universes, where any previous ontological certainties have been abandoned. Shaw notes that the conclusions of many of Borges's texts "call into question one or another of our accepted ideas and beliefs" (2). I suggest that among other thematic elements, the spaces convey the main idea of a metaphysical disorientation. The ambiguous settings radically question any naïve assumption of a stable, reliable world and challenge the characters' ability to make sense of the three-dimensional space around them and of themselves within it. Through the spatial descriptions and the protagonists' perceptions of their surroundings, Borges's writings call into question some of our taken-for-granted ideas and practices of space and make us aware of the medial difficulties or limitations to convey any three-dimensional space in literature.

Few literary critics have studied space in Borges's texts.[1] This may be surprising, since space is a central theme in many of his works. His described *topoi* are never mere static backgrounds or metaphorical spaces. Instead, the seemingly inconspicuous sites become increasingly intricate and active forces. Often, the narrators only indirectly allude to space through the characters' reactions to or excessive iterations of it. The sites transform into riddles, which propel a questioning of spatio-logical certainties.

The topic of space is elaborated in many ways in Borges's work (Bell-Villada, *Borges and His Fiction* 8–12). "Las calles" ("The Streets"), the opening poem of the early collection *Fervor de Buenos Aires* (Passion for Buenos Aires), begins with a meshing of the outside and the inner spaces: "Las calles de Buenos Aires / ya son mi entraña" (*OC* 1: 17). Several of his late poems contain nostalgic creations of a poetical Buenos Aires, revealing an endeavor to enumerate different spaces of the past. In his autobiographically inspired "Elegía" from *El otro, el mismo* (The Other, the Same, 1964), written in Bogotá in 1963, he enumerates many cities he has lived in and describes his unfulfilled yearning to capture a space of his own.

> Oh destino el de Borges,
> haber navegado por los diversos mares del mundo
> o por el único y solitario mar de nombres diversos,
> haber sido una parte de Edimburgo, de Zürich, de las dos Córdobas,
> de Colombia y de Texas,
> haber regresado, a cabo de cambiantes generaciones,
> a las antiguas tierras de su estirpe,
> a Andalucía, a Portugal…
> haber errado por el rojo y tranquilo laberinto de Londres,
> haber envejecido en tantos espejos…
> y no haber visto nada o casi nada
> sino el rostro de una muchacha de Buenos Aires,
> un rostro que no quiere que recuerde… (*OC* 2: 311)

What is a place, asks the poetic voice, but a name, a mere signifier of an absent, perhaps nonexistent signified? For the lyrical instance, the names of the cities become placeholders for various spatial constructs, individual, historical, as well as poetical (the metaphorical "rojo y tranquilo laberinto de Londres" and the metonymical "rostro de una muchacha de Buenos Aires"). The only presence the spaces could possibly acquire is textual, where they may inspire future spatial associations by the readers.

The evocation of space is also a central narrative element in Borges's short stories. Many of the protagonists are characterized by an ardent passion for cartography and geographic research.[2] Several of Borges's preferred symbols are spatial metaphors. One might think about the allusions to the labyrinth, this man-made, artificial world of possibilities, as in the beast's infinite domicile in "La casa de Asterión" or the labyrinthine garden in "El jardín de los senderos que se bifurcan."[3] Another important symbolical space is the library, described in "La Biblioteca de Babel" as an infinite sequence of repeated, hexagonal galleries with reflecting mirrors, multiplying the identical sites.

One of Borges's most intriguing motifs also alludes to a particularly rich space: the aleph. In the short story of the same title, the narrator encounters a minimal spot, containing the whole universe, perceived from any possible viewpoint. He describes how he saw "el aleph, desde todos los puntos, vi en el aleph la tierra, y en la tierra otra vez el aleph y en el aleph la tierra, vi mi cara y mis vísceras, vi tu cara, y sentí vértigo y lloré, porque mis ojos habían visto ese objeto secreto… cuyo nombre usurpan los hombres, pero que ningún hombre ha mirado: el inconcebible universo" (*OC* 1: 625–26). The motif of the aleph, as with many others in Borges, is ambiguous. Although the narrator precisely names the size of the sphere as being a few centimeters in diameter, the evoked space radically subverts any essentialist concept of spatiality. The impetus to measure it is overthrown, since its microcosm has no limits and comprises the macrocosm of the whole universe. The discovery of this paradoxical, unimaginable space is immediately related to the writer's difficulty to render it in a text: "Ahora, al inefable centro de mi relato; empieza, aquí, mi desesperación de escritor… el problema central es irresoluble: la enumeración, siquiera parcial, de un conjunto infinito" (*OC* 1: 624–25). In the here and now of the writing, in the center of the tale, the narrator meditates on the limitations of language to capture and transmit the radical space he has just seen. Similar to the poem quoted above, where the names of cities are described to be placeholders for something absent, the space of the aleph is evoked by a cipher. For the cabbalists, the first letter of the Hebrew alphabet includes all letters, and therefore contains the whole universe (Agheana 177–86). The sphere, seen in the darkness of a dirty cellar in Buenos Aires, exists only as an indication, made of five letters on a page, referring to something, which cannot be represented in the literary act. The narrator only indirectly alludes to the trace of the space's ubiquity and three-dimensionality within the successive structure of language.

While "El aleph" and the poems cited above elaborate on spatial metaphors and the challenge to verbalize a slippery non-space, the short story "La intrusa" presents an unfathomable site that becomes an active character. The story narrates a murder. After the two protagonists have killed the woman they both love, their surroundings change. The dark wasteland around them, "iba agrandándose con la noche" (*OC* 2: 406). In the context of the story, this is not a mental image or hallucinatory impression by the characters, but a description of a characteristic of space itself. The narrator does not give further explanation for the drastic change. This narrative disregard or meager reference to the site may be one of the reasons why these specific spaces in Borges's writings have not received much critical attention. In the following, I will distill the uncanny presence of the *atopos* and its impact for an intermedial aesthetics in Borges's first short story. I read the text as the initial example of this challenging of a fixed space toward a volatile spatiality, which I see as a prominent trend in the writings belonging to the emerging Latin American Boom movement of the 1960s.

According to Emir Rodríguez Monegal, Borges started working on his "Hombre de la esquina rosada" ("Man on Pink Corner") in 1927 and finally published it in 1933, under a pseudonym (27–28). In 1935, he included it in his collection *Historia universal de la infamia* (*A Universal History of Infamy*). Before reading about the life and ethos of the *compadritos*, the tough and violent knife fighters, the readers mentally have to design the space of a painted corner. What does a "pink corner" stand for? Andrew Hurley, in the notes to his translations of Borges's stories, *Collected Fictions, Jorge Luis Borges*, explains that in the Buenos Aires of the beginning twentieth century, many walls were painted with bright pastel colors (530). For those readers who know about the former appearance of the buildings, the cheerful color evokes a Buenos Aires of the past. The corner, according to Hurley, may be interpreted both as an actual street corner and as a generalized neighborhood and hangout of the poor of the slum, possibly on the outskirts of Buenos Aires (530). The pink corner, while mentioned in the title, does not appear in the text itself.

The "man" in the title has no definite article. "Hombre de la esquina rosada" can be an allusion to read the story "visually," which has been suggested by another translator of the text. Pierre Bernès, in the introduction to the French translation of Borges's collected works, published by Gallimard as *Œuvres complètes*, notes: "The title of the original publication, which omits the definite article, reminds the reader of the title of a painting given in the catalogue of an art exhibit. It stresses the graphic aspect of the scene, which Borges, in the preface to the 1935 edition, called the 'pictorial intention' of his work" (qtd. and trans. Hurley, Borges, *Collected Fictions* 530). This resemblance between the title of the story and the title of a visual work opens the text to an intermedial approach. The short story is indeed rife with allusions to the visual, mainly because of the evocations of space. In the prologue of the first edition of *Historia universal de la infamia*, Borges himself pointed out the visual impetus of the short story and noted that the experience of cinema had had a major impact on his writings (*OC* 1: 28). This technique of an initial description of the setting is yet reminiscent of another genre. The terse spatial reference alludes to a stage direction at the beginning of a theater script or filmscript. The title of the short story can be interpreted as a sign for the reader to primarily "set" a mental stage for the fiction to follow.

From the beginning of the story, space is primarily presented as a territory of domination. The narrator describes Francisco Real as an intruder in the microcosm of the slum: "ésos no eran sus barrios porque él sabía tallar más bien por el Norte, por esos laos [*sic*] de la laguna de Guadalupe y de Batería" (*OC* 1: 331). Real challenges the hero of the outskirts, whose power is equally expressed by a spatial metaphor: "Rosendo Juárez el Pegador, era de los que más fuerte pisaban por Villa Santa Rita" (*OC* 1: 331). Juárez is admired by the narrator, because he walks firmly and steps on the place, dominates its inhabitants, and fiercely defends his honor against the slightest offense.

The short story mentions two main spaces: the dancing bar as the social center of the neighborhood of Villa Santa Rita, and the dark outside of the dirty streets. It is in the crowded *milonga* that Real calls out Juárez and dishonors him, and with him, all the inhabitants of the slum. The narrator's inner monologues and clandestine vengeance, on the contrary, take place in the *atopic* outside. The narrative instance refers to the *milonga* as follows: "El salón de Julia… era un galpón de chapas de cinc, entre el camino de Gauna y el Maldonado. Era un local que usté lo divisaba desde lejos, por la luz que mandaba a la redonda el farol sinvergüenza, y por el barullo también" (*OC* 1: 331). Through a deictic device, the narrator places the (fictive) readers in the textual setting. He directly addresses them, when evoking the visual and acoustic quality of the place.

Again, the scene is described in a sensorial and mainly visual manner. The dance whirls the people, divides and reunites them according to its rhythm. The narrator, who is one of them, recalls that "el tango hacía su voluntá con nosotros y nos arriaba y nos perdía y nos ordenaba y nos volvía a encontrar" (*OC* 1: 332). When the intruder enters the bar, all the dancers obsequiously open the way for him. "Los primeros… se abrieron como abanico, apurados" (*OC* 1: 332). Space is used to visualize power. When Juárez refuses Real's challenge, his voice is weak, and does not penetrate space like his opponent's (*OC* 1: 333). The story unfolds almost exclusively through the description of the characters' movements in space. Their physical reactions translate the tension before and during the confrontation.

The narrative voice evokes the main object of desire, the knife, which is in the very center of the coded space. Everybody's eyes are drawn to the glinting sticker in the intruder's hand. "Ahora, le [a Real] relucía un cuchillo en la mano derecha. … Alrededor se habían ido abriendo los que empujaron, y todos los mirábamos a los dos" (*OC* 1: 333). Juárez, on the contrary, remains motionless. His lover, Lujanera, gets his knife out of his pocket and gives it to him. Instead of finally defending himself, he swiftly throws the weapon through an open window, out into the darkness of the Maldonado River, where he himself will hide shortly afterwards. Space, with respect to Juárez, is presented in terms of dispersion and decentering. He first discards his cigarette, later throws away his knife, and finally leaves town: "Agarró el lado más oscuro, el del Maldonado; no lo volví a ver más" (*OC* 1: 334). He disappears into an inscrutable, *atopic* darkness.

The second time the *milonga* is portrayed, it reflects Real's total loss of power. In clear contrast to the first encounter, where he was described as much taller than everybody around him, he is now lying on the floor, while the villagers, forming a circle, are looking down on him. The speaking instance stresses the collective perspective of domination: "El hombre a nuestros pies se moría" (*OC* 1: 335). Borges's narrator evokes the urban battlefield of the *orilleros* in a visual, partly theatrical manner, which translates and reinforces the structures of power. Space "narrates" and interprets the story via its own sign-system (special positions, vectors in the room, the dualistic inside of the *milonga* versus the outside of the Maldonado River).

The second, and much more intriguing and imprecise, site described in "Hombre de la esquina rosada" is the narrator's individual space. He is mainly alone, either in a corner[4] of the bar, or outside in the darkness. When Real enters the bar, the narrator is hit by the swinging door: "Me golpeó la hoja de la puerta al abrirse… [Real] estiró los brazos y me hizo a un lado, como despidiéndose de un estorbo… Me dejó agachado detrás [de la puerta]" (*OC* 1: 332). Ill-treated and humiliated, he leaves the place of confinement after Juárez's dishonor. Outside, while contemplating the infinite sky, he regains self-assurance:

> Me quedé mirando esas cosas de toda la vida—cielo hasta decir basta, el arroyo que se emperraba solo ahí abajo, un caballo dormido, el callejón de tierra, los hornos—y pensé que yo era apenas otro yuyo de esas orillas, criado entre las flores de sapo y las osamentas. ¿Qué iba a salir de esa basura sino nosotros, gritones pero blandos para el castigo…? Sentí después que no, que el barrio cuánto más aporriao [*sic*], más obligación de ser guapo. … Linda al ñudo la noche. Había de estrellas como para marearse mirándolas, unas encima de otras. (*OC* 1: 334)

This description echoes another meditation on man's condition in a similar setting. About 200 years before Borges, Immanuel Kant wrote about two things that would fill the mind with awe: the immense firmament above and the moral law within every human being (*Critique of Practical Reason* 258). Borges's lonesome narrator, admiring the night sky, echoes this dictum. He perceives the grandeur of the firmament in sharp contrast to the shabby surroundings and (differing from Kant's observation) to his inner mediocrity. The contemplation of the vastness strengthens his individual will to face the dreariness and to eventually avenge the humiliation. In this early description, the radical non-space has a positive effect on the character. Its implications will vary in the many literary texts and chapters of this book, yet in all the works chosen, it will possess an immense power over its inhabitants.

The narrator's revenge is carried out in a place that is not described in the short story. Similarly to the theatrical device of something happening "offstage," the text does not focus on how and where the narrator challenges Real. It only briefly mentions that the corpse is thrown into the Maldonado River by the townspeople. Similarly, the narrator's final encounter with La Lujanera is described only indirectly. This scarce evocation of the individual space, in comparison to the detailed description of the social space, is revealing. Borges's story narrates the re-establishment of a common honor system in detail, but does not elaborate on the individual answer to its manifestations, as, for instance, Juárez's decision to leave the slum without fighting or the narrator's compensation for this act. The nameless narrator figuratively reinstalls the codified space of Villa Santa Rita against the intrusion from outside (Real) and the movement away from the slum (Rosendo). In this context, La Lujanera's reaction reaffirms the regulated system. Being the most beautiful woman, she necessarily has to be with the bravest man of the microcosm of the *arrabal* (Cañeque 206–07).

I read this codified space in "Hombre de la esquina rosada" as a literary analogue to Gilles Deleuze and Félix Guattari's concept of the striated, ordered space, as described in *Capitalisme et schizophrénie—Mille plateaux*. Using the example of chess, Deleuze and Guattari describe the space on a chessboard as coded and closed, regulated by strict rules about the occupation of the squares. The critics contrast chess with the game "Go." In "Go," the distribution of space is "smooth" or open, which gives the players the opportunity to create new spaces and to change positions.

> Dans le cas des échecs, il s'agit de se distribuer un espace fermé… d'occuper un maximum de places avec un minimum de pièces.… Les échecs codent et décodent l'espace, tandis que le go procède tout autrement, le territorialise et le déterritorialise (faire du dehors un territoire dans l'espace, consolider ce territoire…, déterritorialiser l'ennemi par éclatement interne de son territoire, se déterritorialiser soi-même en renonçant, en allant ailleurs). (437)

The public space in "Hombre de la esquina rosada," with its fixed code of spatial practice, and the clear hierarchical rules, exemplifies

Deleuze and Guattari's concept of a striated space. Villa Santa Rita has a concise center, the middle of the dance floor of the *milonga.* It is here that the intruder shows his weapon and humiliates the entire slum, represented by the metonymical character Rosendo. In the end, he dies at this place; hence the anterior social and spatial dominance is reaffirmed. In the text, the "smooth," individual space remains dark. The characters only indirectly see the results of the actions that take place there. Borges's narrative over-exposure of the striated space is deceiving. His readers have to read "against the (spatial) grain" in order to discover the partly hidden examples of what I read as a new example of spatiality as an active site of potentiality.

In 1961, the Spanish director Miguel Picazo transformed the five pages of Borges's short story into the 63-minute film *El hombre de la esquina rosada* (The Man on the Pink Corner), produced by Radiotelevisión Española.[5] The simple difference in length, from the few-pages-long story to a film of a duration of more than an hour, already challenges any traditional idea of adaptation based on the concepts of fidelity or illustration of a prior text. *El hombre de la esquina rosada* is the result of an open, intermedial dialogue with the text. In the film, space is less centralized and confined than in the short story. Picazo expands on the scarcely described spaces from the short story.

One of the main narrative changes is that the film has a new protagonist. Instead of the knife fighters, the camera focuses on a female character. Lujanera, who, in the Borges text, only reaffirms the codified system of the male protagonists, has become much more independent and ambiguous. The initial and concluding scenes do not show a man on the pink corner, to which the title alludes, but a woman. Dressed all in black, Lujanera is standing at the lonely street corner, smoking and dreamily gazing over the shabby surroundings. The *mise en scène* of the film is simple. In the opening scene, the poor neighborhood is presented via a few objects: the wash on a clothesline and a plastic curtain in front of a door, fluttering in the wind, sleazy facades, a water bucket, a badly painted street corner, and in the entrance of the house, an electric bulb on a long wire, moved by the wind. The woman's gaze wanders over these objects. All of a sudden, the expression on her face changes and her eyes become sorrowful. The next scene shows a remembered flashback, with two men fighting until one is hurt by the other's knife and falls down. The shot does not show any background or depth. The men are simply moving in the dark, with their faces and bodies scarcely lit, as if they were free from any spatial conditions. In the following shot, back at the street corner, Lujanera realizes that she is observed by a man, the nameless "narrator" (see fig. 1.1). She quickly turns away from him and enters the house.

The interior is a deserted and dark bar, with minimalist equipment: a counter, two stools, some bottles and glasses. It will be the private space of Lujanera and her friend Julia, the bartender. They

Fig. 1.1. Beginning of *El hombre de la esquina rosada* (dir. Miguel Picazo, Radiotelevisión Española, 1961). Lujanera is standing on the street corner, looking at the "narrator."

chat, smoke, and drink *mate* together. Suddenly, they hear voices and the sound of a guitar. Pensively, Lujanera recounts: "Pienso… pienso en las calles en el anochecer… en lo mísero que es todo… un golpe de cuchillo… un hombre bien fornido… muñeco indefenso… lo arrojan al río…y el agua correntosa y sufrida se lo lleva." Lujanera repeats almost literally a sentence from the end of Borges's short story. She meditates languorously: "Noche de estrellas como para marearse mirándola… Mirarla no da sueños… es como una milonga." She starts whistling a *milonga* song, and after a few seconds begins to dance in a sensuous manner, while Julia watches her. While she moves over the dance floor, the dark space around her becomes light. A spotlight follows her, and every place she passes is lighted, until the whole room is brightly lit. The character explores the lonesome bar with her movements; hers is an individual practice of space. Then, the screen goes dark for several seconds. After this sudden narrative cut, the film shows the same bar, now full of people, drinking and dancing in couples, with a little orchestra in the background, which is playing the same song La Lujanera was dancing to.

In the film, the *milonga* is presented in more differentiated ways than in the short story; once, it represents an exclusively female space of confidence and self-expression, another time, it becomes the field of social interaction. Now, after about half the film, Picazo's elaboration closely follows the descriptions of the intruder's challenge and subsequent re-establishment of the former social norm in the short story, highlighting the "striated" characteristic of space. When Real enters, the slamming door hits the "narrator," who remains trapped behind it. Afterwards, the intruder challenges Juárez, whom La Lujanera urges to fight. He resists, throws the knife out of the window, and leaves. Real now dances with La Lujanera. Shortly afterwards, they leave the bar. When they come back, Real is mortally injured, and falls down on the floor. The woman is suspected of having killed him, whereupon the "narrator" steps in to defend her. The dead body of Real is carried out of the bar and thrown into the darkness.

Similar to the text, the film space transmits Real's take-over of the power and his subsequent loss of it, but does so with its own means. The visual medium offers a wide array of possibilities to focus on space. Picazo conveys the codified spaces of dominance mostly through the positions of the camera. The director uses point-of-view shots to convey domination for the scene when Real enters the bar and is looking down on everybody. When Real, later, is lying on the floor, the camera takes the point of view of the bystanders (point-of-view shot, from an extremely high angle), expressing the dominance of the common gaze. The "narrator" steps forward to observe him (the camera focuses on his eyes for several seconds, now from below, from Real's point of view). He arrogantly remarks: "¿Quién hubiera pensado [que] iba a terminar tan bruto en un lugar tan enteramente muerto como éste?" The stranger's defeat is dishonorable, not only because he dies, but even more because he dies at the very center of the microcosm of Villa Santa Rita, literally underneath the slum dwellers' eyes, in the middle of the dance floor in Julia's bar.

Besides the places of domination, the film also focuses on vague non-spaces. In order to invoke them, Picazo uses the less common visual technique of an alternating showing and concealing of certain frames and details of spatial settings. A first example of a space that is sometimes visible, sometimes obscure, is the scene when La Lujanera dances through the dark bar. While she is moving, her surroundings are lighted and become more and more discernible to the viewers. The initially hidden setting opens up and reveals itself to the audience. Her individual practice of space consists of an increasing familiarization with the surroundings. The figures in other vague spaces, however, are at the mercy of their surroundings. Certain places remain entirely dark, such as the surroundings in the two scenes of the knife fighters and the shot when the slum dwellers carry Real's corpse to the river. The viewers see the characters move and consequently infer that they are moving through a three-dimensional setting. However, there is no soil, no horizon, and no other spatial sign around them. Through the technique of showing and concealing of spaces that do not reveal themselves entirely and via the presentation of total darkness on the screen, Picazo's spaces become disconcerting. The "no-color" black conveys the uncertain non-space that the character and viewers cannot identify. Such an inconceivable *atopos* is not openly frightening, but perpetually bewildering, both for the characters within and the external observers in the movie theater. It is puzzling, because of its potentiality, its power to change, to expand, and to swallow the characters from one moment to another.

Picazo combines this technique of an ambivalent, deliberate revealing-hiding with another filmic device, which reinforces the spatial disquiet shown on the screen. All the scenes presenting strange *atopoi* go with specific soundtracks. The voice-overs allude to or directly comment on the spaces of uneasiness. In the scene with the two knife fighters, surrounded by total darkness, the film is accompanied by the voice of a man. Detached from a body, coming itself out of nowhere, this voice meditates on the desolation of certain places, on man's transience, and finally on the mnemotechnic power of sound—the music of a tango—to overcome oblivion.

> ¿Dónde estarán?… quienes [que] ya no son… como si hubiera una región en que el Ayer pudiera ser el Hoy, el Aún y el Todavía… ¿Dónde estará… el malevaje que fundó en polvorientos callejones de tierra o en perdidas poblaciones la secta del cuchillo y del coraje?… Aquellos que pasaron, dejando… a la epopeya un episodio, y que sin odio, lucro o pasión de amor se acuchillaron?… Hay otra brasa, otra candente rosa… Estos muertos viven en el tango… hecho de polvo y tiempo, el hombre dura menos que la liviana melodía… turbio pasado irreal… recuerdo imposible de haber muerto peleando, en una esquina del suburbio. (*OC* 2: 266–67)

The voice recites Borges's poem "El tango," written about thirty years after the short story, and included in the collection *El otro, el mismo* [1964].[6] Basing his scene on the author's technique of the intertextual linkage, Picazo now transposes the textual interplay to the literary medium and includes the poem in his film on a short story by the Argentinean author.

In the intermedial dialogue of the tango's text with the film, the poem comments on the images shown on the screen. The voice mentions the dreary outskirts, lost in a nowhere place. Similar to the title of the short story, it also names a poor street corner. While the two knife fighters are shown on the screen, the voice recites[7] the following two stanzas:

> En un instante que hoy emerge aislado,
> Sin antes ni después, contra el olvido,
> Y que tiene el sabor de lo perdido,
> De lo perdido y recuperado.
>
> En los acordes hay antiguas cosas:
> El otro patio y la entrevista parra.
> (Detrás de las paredes recelosas
> El Sur guarda un puñal y una guitarra.) (*OC* 2: 266–67)

The film illustrates the past moment, to which the speaker alludes. Besides the human voice, Picazo also adds the low melody of a tango. As if the music, both mentioned by the voice and present as a background song, had the power to conjure the scene of the past fight, it then appears on the screen. But the images, although they are visible in the here and now of the film, still convey the idea of a lost presence. They do so via the representation of negative or absent spaces. The partly hidden space is an active character, as the poem evokes it: "Detrás de las paredes recelosas, el Sur guarda un puñal y una guitarra." This negative *atopos* even has the power to devour the character, as the last scene will demonstrate.

The final scene that shows a spatial "non-setting" is the one when the slum dwellers carry Real's dead body out of the bar and throw it into the river. Again, Picazo adds a voice-over to comment on the desecrators' atrocious labor. Julia's voice narrates: "Un hombre alto, fornido y un golpe de cuchillo… este hombre ya no es nada… le arrancan las vísceras… Y el agua torrentosa se lo lleva." In the short story, the allusions to this carnage are vague. The narrator claims not to be sure about what happens with the corpse, since, as he says, he did not want to see it (*OC* 1: 336). The spectators of the film are not as free to look away and to speculate about whether or not the corpse was mutilated. When Julia's voice pronounces the sentence "le arrancan las vísceras," the screen shows this act of gutting. The camera zooms in on the wide open, bleeding body with the dead man's innards exposed. Again, this brutally exposed detail is not presented in any spatial relation. The image centers on the mutilated intestines in bright colors, but does not include any three-dimensional references, as for instance the body or the surrounding space. For more than ten seconds, the screen shows this detailed close-up on a man's innards, with several hands and knives cutting and ripping them off (see fig. 1.2). At the end, when the voice recounts that "el agua torrentosa se lo lleva," the screen shows several hands that are throwing the corpse somewhere. There is no river, but again, an entirely black area, where Real's body disappears after a few seconds. The audience is left alone with a black screen that shows nothing.

Picazo took up Borges's invitation to confabulate on a site of no traditional spatial characteristics. In his cinematographic elaboration, space is evoked in more diverse ways than in the short story. Besides portraying a centralized place of confinement and male domination, the director also shows places of individual freedom and artistic creativity (Lujanera's solitary dance). Finally, the camera focuses on vague, disconcerting spaces, partly hidden, partly revealed. Most radically, these spaces are presented as entirely black areas on the screen. While the narrator in Borges's text meditates on the shabby slum of spatial confinement and contrasts it with the starry firmament above, Picazo's film does not show any bright points of reference. Instead, it presents blurring or

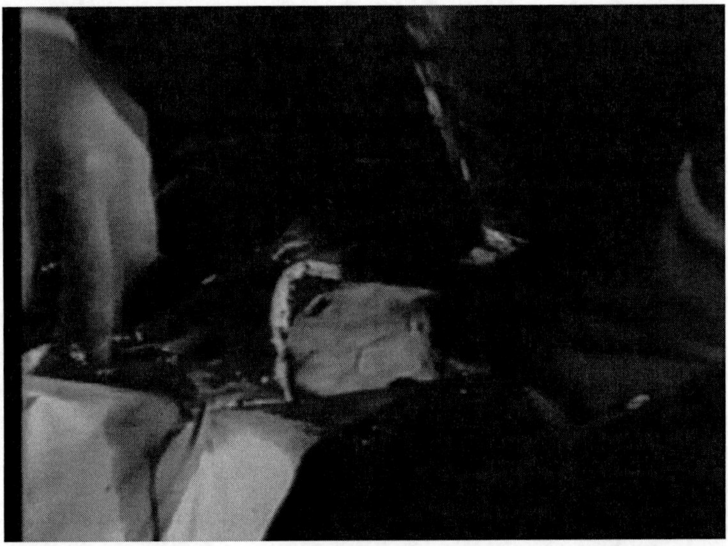

Fig. 1.2. Close-up of Real's innards from the end of *El hombre de la esquina rosada* (dir. Miguel Picazo, Radiotelevisión Española, 1961).

confusing black areas on the screen. Similar to black holes in the universe, these dark areas ask the viewers a riddle. They are active, but invisible (even light cannot escape them); and they possess an immense force of attraction. Here, we are reminded of Augé's description of the *atopos*: "Ce qui est significatif dans l'expérience du non-lieu, c'est sa force d'attraction [contre les] pesanteurs du lieu et de la tradition" (147). At the end of the film, the dark holes even devour the intruder Real, being the final force to reinstall the former hierarchy in Villa Santa Rita. While the short story evokes a lost space of a crime out of nowhere, the film radicalizes the spatial relativity. Except for Lujanera's individual exploring of the black *atopoi*, these spaces illustrate the overall deep existential disquiet of the characters. They are presented to be accidentally in or away from these environments. This random being in an active space is addressed right from the beginning of the film. The initial words refer to the "lost" characters in a space: "¿Dónde estarán?" asks the voice-over with Borges's words. Space, besides being described as a disconcerting force by the characters and the disembodied voice, is also visually shown as a troubling setting, sometimes concealed, sometimes entirely dark and devouring.

Chapter Two

The Power of Staging

Spaces of Emulation in Jorge Luis Borges's "Tema del traidor y del héroe" and Bernardo Bertolucci's *Strategia del ragno*

Borges's "Tema del traidor y del héroe" ("Theme of the Traitor and the Hero") has received much critical attention since its first publication in 1944. From its beginning, the three-page story is clearly marked as a self-referential artifice, an artistic work in progress. The narrator considers writing, perhaps, the theme, which, at this point, he barely sees: "He imaginado este argumento, que escribiré tal vez. … Faltan pormenores, rectificaciones, ajustes; hay zonas de la historia que no me fueron reveladas aún; hoy, 3 de enero de 1944, la vislumbro así" (*OC* 1: 496). However, while he writes about his decision to put the theme to paper or not, the story itself has already begun. In this short text, space is a deliberately ambiguous concept, yet rich in connotations. The narrative voice presents the setting as a choice among a wide range of alternative timeframes and places. After discussing a number of possible settings, the narrator, seemingly in an offhand manner, chooses Ireland: "La acción trascurre en un país oprimido y tenaz: Polonia, Irlanda, la república de Venecia, algún estado sudamericano o balcánico. … Ha transcurrido, mejor dicho. … Digamos (para comodidad narrativa) Irlanda; digamos 1824" (*OC* 1: 496).

Ireland and the 1820s are supposedly selected for convenience's sake.[1] After addressing the readers and apparently including them in the process and after discussing the place and time of the action, this initial narrator, in 1944, designates a narrator of the drama to be recounted: In 1924, Ryan, the great-grandson of a martyr of the Irish rebellion, is doing research for a biography of his ancestor, which he plans to publish on the occasion of the centenary of Kilpatrick's death. A third narrative frame opens, where the readers learn about Ryan's great-grandfather, Fergus Kilpatrick, the venerated hero of the Irish national movement who was murdered in 1824. Ryan investigates some enigmatic facts about his ancestor's death, and discovers that the supposed hero was in fact a traitor, who was killed by his comrades, after having signed his own death sentence. Since the revelation of Kilpatrick's treachery and a following execution would have harmed the rebellion, Kilpatrick's assistant Nolan made a plan to convert the traitor's execution into an instrument that fostered the political cause. Nolan was an expert in Shakespearian drama as well as vast theatrical performances (*Festspiele*) played in public spaces that require hundreds of actors. He meticulously planned and staged the execution as an assassination by the British opponents. Ryan notes:

> Kilpatrick fue ultimado en un teatro, pero de teatro hizo también la entera ciudad. ... El condenado entró en Dublín, discutió, obró, rezó, reprobó, pronunció palabras patéticas, y cada uno de esos actos que reflejaría la gloria, había sido prefigurado por Nolan. Centenares de actores colaboraron con el protagonista; el rol de algunos fue complejo, el de otros momentáneo. ... Así fue desplegándose en el tiempo el populoso drama, hasta que el 6 de agosto de 1824, en un palacio de funerarias cortinas que prefiguraba el de Lincoln, un balazo anhelado entró en el pecho del traidor y del héroe, que apenas pudo articular, entre dos efusiones de brusca sangre, algunas palabras previstas. (*OC* 1: 497–98)

Dublin becomes a stage, where Fergus Kilpatrick and everybody he meets during his last days perform according to Nolan's script.[2] The traitor, playing the role of the hero, is murdered in a dramatic way in the place of spectacle *par excellence*, the theater. While sitting in the audience of the theater, he subverts the spatial boundaries between stage and auditorium by acting out his personal drama, surrounded by a newly created audience (the former audience and the actors onstage). In contrast to the emulating action on the pre-defined stage, his acting is now performative, to borrow Austin's term.

Nolan's plot, besides transcending ordinary spatial restrictions (such as the division between a stage and an audience) also transcends temporal units. His screenplay repeats numerous passages and motifs from Shakespeare's *Julius Caesar* and *Macbeth*.[3] The settings and motifs that imitate earlier fictions help Ryan discover the truth about his great-grandfather, behind the mask of the national hero. He speculates that these hints were provided on purpose, that the cautious choreographer and stage director Nolan had foreseen an investigation for the future. One hundred years after Kilpatrick's martyrdom and rightful punishment were acted out and performed, the great-grandson realizes that the drama is still continuing and that even he plays a role in it. The story ends as follows: "Ryan sospecha que el autor los [los pasajes imitados de Shakespeare] intercaló para que una persona, en el porvenir, diera con la verdad. Comprende que él también forma parte de la trama de Nolan. … [Ryan] resuelve silenciar el descubrimiento. Publica un libro dedicado a la gloria del héroe; también eso, tal vez, estaba previsto" (*OC* 1: 498). The dubitative *tal vez* from the initial sentence is repeated several times in the text and again in the final phrase. The story opens and closes with a strong skepticism as to its own status of enunciation, which reinforces its artificial and unfinished state. Etymologically, the adverb *tal vez* also alludes to the motif of iteration and repetition that is elaborated throughout the short story. Borges does not choose terms such as *posiblemente, puede que*, or *quizás. Tal vez,* in its literal sense, conveys the idea of a particular or present (*tal*) turn or instance (*vez*). On the microlevel of this little semantic unit, the narrative description of a murder in a public space is presented as "a particular turn" among other past, present, and future presentations, such as a drama by Shakespeare or the historical assassination of Abraham Lincoln.

In this text about the fictional and performative power of a performance on a stage, language itself alludes to the visual, dramatic art. Some paragraphs read almost like stage directions. The narrator describes places, colors, and situations in short, simple sentences. Ryan's and Kilpatrick's actions are evoked in repetitive, anaphoric syntagmatic units, reminiscent of a heroic, dramatic style. According to Ulrich Wicks, "Borges' text does not really represent the story it presents; it is synoptic and almost reads like a scenario, something to be represented. … In Borges' text, 'the action takes place'" (26). Many verbs allude to the semantic field of seeing, such as "he imaginado," "me fue revelado," and "vislumbro" from the beginning of the text, or its last word "previsto." The narrator Ryan refers to the story as to something visual in front of someone's eyes. Through this reference to the visual sense, he invites the readers to mentally set a stage of an "Ireland" and a "theater" for themselves.

Besides stylistic affinities to stage directions and allusions to visual presentations, the literary text also refers to theater through the explicit description of the roles the characters have to play. This role playing is already discernible in the changing voices (active to passive forms) of the verbs mentioned above. A striking shift takes place from the active forms in the beginning to the past participle at the end. The initial narrator first has "imaginado," then affirms that "me fue revelado" and is finally able to "vislumbr[ar]." Ryan, on the contrary, is dependent on an unnamed, provident force ("publica un libro dedicado a la gloria del héroe…, también eso, tal vez, estaba previsto"). He perceives himself as an actor, who performs a previously arranged, pre-seen plot, which might be repeated many times, as the imperfect tense suggests.

The first narrative voice, similar to a stage director, casts Ryan and presents him as the further narrator. Ryan's position shifts, since he is also, in other moments of the short story, a character, the author of a further text, and the possible reincarnation of the hero-traitor. Kilpatrick, the former hero, turned traitor, switches roles, too, when he (re)incarnates the heroic model for the Irish people. Emir Rodríguez Monegal stresses this characteristic and defines Kilpatrick as a theatrical *homo duplex*: "[El relato] duplica al personaje al victimizarlo y hacerle cambiar de papel" (*Conversaciones sobre Borges* 36). Forced to change roles, Kilpatrick is both a hero and a traitor, depending on the position of the observers (the conspirators, the Irish people, or the audience in the movie theater) as well as on the moment of his performance on the narrative "stage."

The text deconstructs the clear spatial definitions and boundaries the readers have come to accept for literary and dramatic works. Kilpatrick is killed in a theater, surrounded by hundreds of actors and extras, most of them unaware of their participation in the drama. The site of his presented, as well as executed, assassination is not the stage, but the audience, which is normally a place of silent meditation. The traitor-hero's death takes place in the inactive counterpart to the stage. Kilpatrick literally dies offstage amidst the spectators, who all expect the drama to be acted out at the designated place of representation, which is the stage. The traitor-hero is punished-martyred on a newly defined stage, different from the conventional space of dramatic emulation. The place where Kilpatrick dies conditions the audience's interpretation of the act. When he is killed, he is amidst the spectators. Hence, according to the audience, he is as passive and innocent as any other viewer. Borges's Nolan proves that a fine-tuned screenplay and a thoughtfully chosen place may convert a traitor into a hero in the eyes of the surrounding spectators and future narrators of the event. Space becomes a powerful maker of the metafictional quality of the text. In the present text, the *atopos* contains several sites. It emerges from spatio-temporal juxtapositions, where, among others, the notions of a foreground and a background, the concept of the scene and the ob-scene, are blurred. Similar to an Escher painting, the distinct forms and settings fuse like pieces of a puzzle. The "user" of such a space, or the reading observer, however, cannot perceive the different pieces simultaneously, but has to "leap" from one staging to the other. Again, the active, ambiguous non-space itself points toward a collapse of spatial certainties.

In the 1960s, most of Borges's works were translated into French, English and Italian.[4] They were widely cited in critical and creative texts in the United States and Europe. French director Jacques Rivette, for instance, in one of the opening scenes of *Paris nous appartient* (*Paris Belongs to Us*) [1961], shows a copy of *Enquêtes* (*Other Inquisitions*), lying on the heroine's bedside table. Filmmaker Jean-Luc Godard covertly cites Borges in the last sequence of *Alphaville* [1965], when the computer Alpha 60, in his final combat with the hero, spews some lines of Borges's "Nueva refutación del tiempo" ("A New Refutation of Time") (Cozarinsky 88). The critic and novelist Claude Ollier (who wrote a critique of Rivette's film[5]) publishes the novel *L'échec de Nolan* (Nolan's Failure) in 1967, where he elaborates on the character of the former detective and stage director of Borges's "Tema del traidor y del héroe." Italian director Bernardo Bertolucci is another of the many artists who use Borges's text as a source for their own artistic creations.

In 1970, Bertolucci made the film *Strategia del ragno* (*The Spider's Strategy*). He explicitly mentioned Borges's short story in the opening credits: according to its director, the work is "liberamente ispirata dal racconto 'Tema del tradittore e dell'eroe' di J. L. Borges" ("freely inspired by the story 'The Theme of the Traitor and the Hero' by J. L. Borges").[6] The short story constitutes a point of departure for the latter artist's own creative work for the cinematographic screen. Due to its brief and schematic plot outline, the literary text is itself open to further elaborations. Borges's tentative "digamos (para comodidad narrativa) Irlanda;

digamos 1824" (*OC* 1: 496) invites the reader to speculate about other places and times. Bertolucci chooses Italy in the 1930s as the setting for his version of the traitor-hero. He replaces Dublin with an Italian town in the Po Valley, called Tara. In the film, the characters of Borges's Ryan and his great-grandfather Kilpatrick become Athos Magnani and his father Athos Magnani, the latter a local anti-Fascist hero who was killed by the Italian Fascists.[7]

Bertolucci's plot is less abstract and ambiguous than Borges's. However, I do not read Borges's narrator's initial pondering about possible plots as a coquettish escape from "situatedness" and fear of taking a stand on political realities. Instead, I interpret it as a bitter, ethical remark on man's regression into violence for a supposedly good cause (with the *topos* of the Irish noble rebel), with too many negative examples to choose from. In addition, I do not interpret the actual selection of the plot as merely accidental: Borges's narrator eloquently covers up the fact that after having been torn between numerous options, he did make a choice. Although less obviously than in the case of the space presented by Bertolucci, Borges's selection of Dublin in 1824, 1924, and 1944 can be justified on numerous levels. The city has been one of the most contested sites in Britain and Ireland. It has also served as the "spatial muse" for various fictions about emulation and mirroring, among them, most prominently, James Joyce's *Ulysses*.

The director embeds the story in the political context of Fascism in Italy in the 1930s. As Eugenio Bolongaro notes, "Tara is not far from Pavia, a detail that situates the narrative within a specific geographical and historical context: we are in a region of Italy (the Emilia-Romagna) that was the breeding ground for Fascism and anti-Fascism, as well as the theatre of a great deal of political violence before, during, and after Mussolini's regime" (76). As in the Borges text, the place of the assassination in the film is a theater. But while Borges does not mention the actual drama performed onstage when Kilpatrick dies, in the film, Athos Sr. is assassinated during the presentation of Guiseppe Verdi's opera *Rigoletto*, more precisely the aria "Maledizione." This same music is also climactic for Athos Jr., thirty years after the father's death. He discovers the truth about the hero's feigned martyrdom, sitting in a loge of Tara's theater, while listening to the opera about a betrayal and a staged murder.[8]

Athos Jr. is summoned by his father's former mistress, Draifa, to carry out the investigation in 1960. He is quickly caught in a net of ambiguities pertaining to the myth of Athos Sr., who is vigorously defended by the townspeople. In this plot, there are also Shakespearian elements as in Borges's story. It is due to these fictional clues that Athos Jr. discovers that his father had been a traitor. Athos Sr. had developed this scenario, together with his three friends (Borges's Nolan is replaced by three villagers), but had then informed the Fascist authorities of the plot to kill Mussolini during a visit to the town, at a performance of *Rigoletto*. When he is found out, he decides to have his friends kill him instead of Mussolini (in the text, it is Nolan who proposes this plot to the supposed hero). Thirty years later, the son plans to reveal the imposture at a ceremony commemorating the anniversary of Athos Sr.'s death. After he realizes that he himself plays a role in this drama, he conceals the truth and ends up delivering a panegyric to his father.

Like the short story, the film *Strategia del ragno* presents various stages, spaces of emulation, and metafictional inquiry that are often inserted one into the other. Like Borges, Bertolucci opens his work with a self-reflexive remark on fiction making itself, now referring to the cinematographic genre: After an initial shot of almost a full turn, showing green fields, an undulating hilly landscape, and railroad tracks, the movement of the camera stops. For several seconds, it focuses on a station with an incoming train. This shot is reminiscent of one of the first moments in film: the Lumière Brothers' 50-second film, *Arrivée d'un train à la Ciotat* (*Arrival of a Train at La Ciotat Station*), from 1895 (Bolongaro 75). Bertolucci, at the beginning of his filmic narration, alludes to one of the first *mises en scène* in the cinematographic medium.[9] After the train has come to a halt, a young man and a sailor descend, take their bags, leave the station, and walk toward the camera. The young man is Athos Jr., the protagonist of the film. The sailor, a puzzling character, only appears at the very beginning and end of the film. For Ulrich Wicks, in his analysis of *Strategia del ragno*, the sailor refers to the work's medial self-reflexivity. Wicks compares him to the audience in a movie theater, who is about to see the film:

> The sailor… is functional only on the discursive level—he is the viewer. … The thud of his pack [thrown out of the train] is our investment in the story just as it starts. … In the second shot, the sailor is meandering behind Athos… then, he sits down on a bench (as we sit in our movie seat?), opens his arms, and

> says "Tara!" as though to say, "Here is your stage; let your story begin." The next shot is the first use of the displaced diegetic insert: the theater dominating Tara. (32)

The sailor does what the viewers in the movie theater are about to do. The tracks of the railroad at the beginning and the end of the movie are means of entering and leaving the filmic stage of Tara, or, taking into account the title of the movie, entering and escaping the fictional spider's web.

The name of the village, repeated many times in the film by the characters and shown on street signs, is polyvalent. As Sante Matteo points out, the word *tara* in Italian has three meanings, all of which might suggest what the town represents in the film. The first is the noun *tare,* referring to the gross weight of a package. *Tare,* with respect to the storyline, corresponds to the "packaging" of Athos Sr.'s myth, the web of lies and legends the son has to break through to reveal yet another layer of signification we may want to call its "truth." The second meaning of the noun in Italian is a hereditary illness or defect. And in fact, Athos Jr. is increasingly overwhelmed by the same dilemmas that afflicted his father, such as the emotion of claustrophobia and the attempt to run away from a truth he does not want to face. Several times, the camera shows the characters running away from Tara and its inhabitants, rushing through the woods. It is sometimes difficult for the viewers to distinguish the father from the son, since both are played by the same actor (Giulio Brogi) and both *personae* wear similar clothes. Third, *Tara* might refer to the verb *tarare,* which determines the correspondence between an instrument of measurement and a determined object to be measured. This meaning, Matteo argues, "would allude to the film's self-referential quality, its exploration of its own relationship to what it is trying to represent. … The film explores (*tarare*) how cinema, as an art and as an instrument of measuring and mapping reality, is implicated in and determined by the history and the fictions it tries to depict" (28). Eugenio Bolongaro points out another signification, which refers back to the title of the film: "'Tara'… is composed of the first two syllables of the most feared spider found in Italy (the tarantula) as well as of the famous dance that both manifests and attempts to fight off the paralyzing effect of its bite (the tarantella)" (76). I would like to add two more interpretations of the name. According to the *Encyclopaedia Britannica*, *Tara* describes an ancient Irish royal residence with circular earthworks, which occupies a key place in Irish legend and history. In 1843, the hill of Tara was the site of an important Irish republican meeting. Choosing this name might be Bertolucci's way of linking his Italy with the Ireland described in the Borges story.[10] The name of the town possibly refers to yet another cinematographic work. For viewers of Hollywood films from the 1950s, *Tara* is also the name of the plantation in *Gone with the Wind*, a film about memory and about a national trauma just as is Bertolucci's. As in *Gone with the Wind*, *Strategia del ragno* is about a civil war; it also deals with the conflict between political duties and individual passions, and evolves toward a final loss.

Similarly to Borges in the literary text, Bertolucci presents the techniques and processes of cinematographic fictionalization in his film. The work of art is made and unmade before the eyes of readers and viewers. Among other elements, both artists convey the theme of a self-reflexive work through their evocations and presentations of exchangeable non-spaces, that all challenge spatial conventions, such as the blurring of the distinction between an audience and a stage.

Bertolucci's cinematographic Tara looks like a theater scene: the spatial elements are arranged very homogeneously and symmetrically.[11] Matteo describes the city as an artificial, previously arranged place: "There is something a little too homogeneous about the setting. It looks and feels theatrical. … It seems a little too perfect, too symmetrical, too uncluttered; a stage, and also a spider's web: empty, suspended in time and place; waiting to ensnare the spider's next prey" (18). The young man walks along deserted streets, rectangular places, through symmetrical porticoes with sharp shadow and light alternation. The camera follows him at a distance, with long tracking shots. The film about a search has many sequences of the protagonist walking through a bleak scenario, peering out at nothing, with the camera behind him. Athos Jr., the reluctant investigator of his father's death, inspects the site of the crime and encounters many symbols and inscriptions in the space. They all repeat the same name. He stares at the street sign on a wall: "Via Athos Magnani" (Athos Magnani Street). (The camera reads the sign from right to left. This reading backward may be another metafictional device, signaling that Athos Jr. is on a journey back, marked by signs and different ways of reading and interpreting them.) He walks along the "Albergo Athos Magnani"

(Hotel Athos Magnani). He also looks at the bust of a man, highly similar to himself. Again, the inscription on the pedestal repeats the same name. Finally, the young man observes a tombstone, with a photograph, a date of birth and of death, and the inscription "Athos Magnani. Eroe vigliaccamente assassinato dal piombo fascista" (Athos Magnani. A hero perfidiously murdered by a Fascist bullet). With its arcades, facades, statues, and gravestones, Tara is a memorial place of Athos Sr.'s past glory.

The house of the father's former mistress reinforces the site's atmosphere of past liveliness. Draifa[12] lives in an immense vine-covered villa, with its shutters closed, reminiscent of an enchanted castle. Similarly, the railroad tracks, at the end of the film, are overgrown with weeds, suggesting that the place has not been in contact with other towns for a long time.[13] Tara is a site of stasis, made of letters, signs, and stone, which seems frozen in nostalgia, with its inhabitants[14] constantly evoking Athos Sr.'s life.[15] The son is the only character who at least initially moves and actively occupies space. He is a stranger who comes to Tara from Milan with a precise aim: he wants to meet his father's former mistress, who has sent for him. He asks for the way to her house, gets on a bicycle, and arrives at the place. Several times, he wants to leave and announces that he soon has to catch the train back to Milan.[16] But increasingly, the surroundings entrap him. When he returns to his hostel after the first visit at Draifa's house, he passes through a dark tunnel, scarcely illuminated by a light bulb on the ceiling. The camera is situated in the middle of the road, focusing on Athos Jr. on the bicycle from a distance. Two men appear, on both margins of the filmed image, facing each other (the camera shows their black silhouettes and the upper parts of their bodies), and start to argue and move their hands in threatening gestures. They do not pay attention to Athos Jr., and do not move to facilitate his passage. He almost has to squeeze between them in order to pass. This is the first of many spaces of confinement he encounters. He is also trapped in a horse stable, as well as in several rooms, on the central plaza, when the villagers surround him, and finally at the station, waiting for a train that will most likely never arrive. Bertolucci shows the character's spatial, ideological, and epistemological captivity more clearly than Borges.

Another setting embodies Athos Jr.'s entrapment in even more salient ways: Several times, the camera films him through a series of window and door frames. When he enters Draifa's house for the second time, the camera is positioned in the room where she is waiting for him. After entering the house through the main entrance, he has to pass through two doors to get to her. Similarly, his father, while watching outside from Draifa's room, is shot by the camera through a window and a door frame. These shots convey the idea of a telescopic sight, aiming at the character in the center. In one of the final shots, Athos Jr. is standing outside the train station and is filmed through the doors and window frames from the other side of the building. The viewer's gaze is directed toward the center of the setting. The father and the son, inserted into their surroundings, are trapped in sequences of black frames, like insects caught in the web of a spider, as alluded to by the title of the film. I read the image of a set of parallel frames as a visual analogy to a quote from Borges's short story. In the text, the narrator compares the parallelisms between his great-grandfather's death and the deaths of several characters of Shakespearian drama with an abstract design of parallel lines. "Esos paralelismos… inducen a Ryan a suponer… un dibujo de líneas que se repiten" (*OC* 1: 497). Bertolucci gives a visual equivalent of the pattern of repeated lines, when he presents father and son in similar shots, both surrounded by several layers of parallel framings. Each line, each framing, which is added to the pattern refers to the repetition of a motif (such as the pre-arranged assassination of a man) in a different spatial and temporal setting.[17] Ryan, Kilpatrick, Athos Jr., and Athos Sr. are placed inside a specific arrangement of recurring events, and, hence, they are figuratively framed by previous enactments of a drama that becomes in turn their own.

The cinematographic presentation of this design adds yet another frame to the ones shown in the shots. Bertolucci carefully positions the frame segments when showing Athos Jr. and Sr. in the middle of several framings. The margins of the images on the screen are again parallel to the inner frames of the shots. The traditional bar of separation between the artistic elaboration (the film) and the outside (the wall upon which it is projected) is incorporated into the broader pattern of repeating frames, focusing on a character. For the viewers, Athos Jr. and Sr. are not only trapped between door and window frames; they are also arrested by the sequential photos on the celluloid strip, reeling off during the presentation of the film. The viewer in the movie theater, similar to a spider peering at its web, focuses on the character, presented in a set of parallel frames or fibres of the animal's web. In this way, Athos Jr. and Sr. become visual fares for avid moviegoers.

Besides showing clearly marked, three-dimensional spaces of emulation, Bertolucci also presents two-dimensional reflections of primary spaces. He does so with the help of mirrors. Like Borges in many of his writings,[18] Bertolucci demonstrates his fascination with mirrors, with their capacity to reflect and insert projections of other spaces into a present setting, and to multiply, blur, and refract images. The Italian word *spettacolo* designating an artistic representation (Lat. *spectaculum*, echoed in the English *spectacle*) such as theater, opera, or film has the same root as *specchio*, the Italian word for mirror (Lat. *speculum*). Both terms derive from the Latin verb *spicere*, "to see, view, observe, or project with the eye" (Lat. *oculus*). *Spettacolo* and *specchio* both evoke a secondary visual representation, either in a designated space, such as the theater stage, or on a surface, the two-dimensional reduction of a space in a mirror. In the film, Bertolucci elaborates on both these elements, in the three-dimensional presentation on a stage (Tara, the theater, the framings, etc.), as well as the two-dimensional reflection of a setting. Like the stage, the image in a mirror adds a projected space to a present surrounding (Kestner 100–07). *Strategia del ragno* shows many shots where a single point of view is broken up through the insertion of other images that are reflected in a mirror.

According to Marc Augé, the reflecting surface is a key element of the supermodern *atopos*, as for instance in airports or shopping malls. It deludes the users into thinking that they can find and even inscribe themselves in the impersonal settings. Yet the reflection is highly ambiguous: "C'est avec une image de lui-même que [le voyageur] se trouve confronté en définitif, mais une bien étrange image en vérité. Le seul visage qui se dessine, … [c'est le] visage… d'une solitude d'autant plus déroutante qu'elle en évoque des millions d'autres… le passager des non-lieux fait l'expérience… du présent perpétuel" (129–31). Similarly, Tara's time does not progress, and Athos Jr., when looking at a mirror, cannot perceive himself as a single identity, but as a changing sequence of reflections.

In a scene where Athos Jr. is washing his face, he is filmed through a little mirror that is attached to a commode in the middle of the room, while the boy of the hostel is watching him.

This shot shows the face of the boy and Athos Jr.'s face, turned to the child, reflected in the mirror, as well as the back of Athos's head and the surrounding space behind him. The field of vision of the film camera is made up of two opposing perspectives. The mirror, in this sequence, is a tool that multiplies the points of views of the camera and, therefore, enriches the observer's vision. Here, the reflected image enhances perception. Besides this positive presentation of a mirror as a perception-altering device, *Strategia del ragno* also presents more confusing and disconcerting kinds of reflections. An example is a scene with Draifa, filmed next to a bunch of flowers. At the beginning, the shot does not show the frame of the mirror or the surrounding space. After a few seconds, when the camera moves backward, the viewers (Athos Jr. and the audience in the movie theater) recognize that the image they have been looking at was not a direct recording of a space, but of its reflection in a mirror. Athos Jr., when entering the room, first looks to his right, and then makes a turn to the left, after the camera reveals that the filmed image was a reflection in a mirror. This turn suggests that the character has been misguided, thinking that Draifa would stand at his right, where there is only a reflecting surface. Just as Athos Jr. has to turn around, the extradiegetic viewers in the cinema have to readjust their imagined spatial arrangement (a 180° turn) and "shift" the apparently homogeneous and fixed space. Space becomes a relative reflection of a setting (located opposite the mirror) inserted into yet another setting (the site where the mirror is placed). In this sequence, the mirror makes the viewers aware of the versatility of a projected space, of its merely relative arrangement.

The most elaborate use of a mirror in the film is the sequence of the hero-traitor's death and his son's discovery of the circumstances thirty years later. When Athos Sr. plans his own murder/assassination, he relies on the procedure of a public spectacle and uses the device of a mirror (joining the *spettacolo* and the *specchio*) to reach his goal. He tells his friends: "Offriremo uno *spettacolo* di una morte *drammatica*... una morte leggendaria di un eroe... Proseguiremo *come nel teatro*. Tutto il popolo di Tara parteciperà senza saperlo" [my emphasis] ("We will offer the *spectacle* of a *dramatic* death... the legendary death of a hero... Let's proceed *like in the theater*. The whole village of Tara will participate without knowing"). The box in the theater where Athos Sr. is to be killed is equipped with a mirror (see fig. 2.1). He simultaneously watches the presentation of *Rigoletto* (in front of him, as a spectator) and the door behind him (as an actor of his personal drama), so that he will not miss his friends when they enter to shoot him in the back, as planned in advance. Initially, Athos Sr. only sees his own mirror image (shown on the screen). The reason why he is staring at it is to see a reflection he has staged and imagined in advance (of his three friends entering the box to shoot him). In this scene, the mirror is used to reflect the accomplishment of a projected vision. The longed-for reflection of the friends/murderers in the mirror will finally testify that Athos's mental foreshadowing of the *spettacolo* of his death has been acted out. The image in the mirror is a *déjà vu* of the traitor-hero's mentally anticipated creation of the same image.

The son, thirty years later, finds out about the details of his father's assassination and martyrdom while sitting in the same box and looking in the same mirror. Initially, he wonders why his

Fig. 2.1. Still from *Strategia del ragno* (dir. Bernardo Bertolucci, Radiotelevisione Italiana, 1970) with Athos Sr. looking at his mirror image in the theater box, before being killed.

father did not defend himself, since he must have seen the assassin approaching from behind. Then, he wakes up to the idea that Athos Sr. had actually conceived his own murder. The mirror setting allows the son to reconstruct the past event and to create the visual image of a "pas encore vu." The image Athos Jr. is projecting onto the mirror makes him aware of a past occurrence (his father's death), whereas the image projected by the father had been a foreshadowing of a future event (his death). In both scenes, the mirror does not show the act itself; it is a surface for the father's and the son's creative projections and opens up a homogeneous spatio-temporal setting (in 1930 and 1960, respectively). Its reflection, whose presence is included in the same space, introduces an additional situation. The father and the son, sitting in the box of the theater, listening to the music of *Rigoletto*, are projecting the same action in the very same place. The box and the mirror guide the characters to develop their respective inner images of the future and the past, in one foreshadowing a scene, in another reconstructing it. Besides their different functions, all the mirrors shown in *Strategia del ragno* allude to additional spaces within a present setting. As soon as there is reflection, a fixed setting is broken up, dispersed, and multiplied. The characters are no longer entirely within a uniform surrounding. Space becomes less reliable, both for the characters (for Athos Sr. and even more so for the reluctant investigator, Athos Jr.) and for the audience.

At the end of the film, the camera focuses on the Renaissance tower of Tara. This building has already been shown several times from a distance. During previous shots with the whole village from different angles, the tower was always in the very middle of the frame, emphasizing its central position with respect to the surroundings. Athos Sr., before being killed, wishes to climb the tower, "per vedere Tara dall'alto" ("to see Tara from above"). Through the panoramic view from an elevated distance, he attempts to perceive and understand the three-dimensional setting, and to dominate the place with what remains to him, his gaze. An overlook signals detachment and distance from everyday life. In many cases, it is a sign of power. However, Athos Sr.'s visit to the tower with his panoramic vision does not convey any power. On the contrary, it manifests his total loss of power over the place and its inhabitants. Bertolucci's camera mounts with the character, films the overview, but at the same time, shows Athos Sr. as a pure silhouette without any characteristic features or corporality (see fig. 2.2). He is reduced to a black figure in front of Tara, a pure abstract and replaceable form. Bertolucci presents a *persona*, lacking any signs of individuation.

Fig. 2.2. Athos Sr. as a pure silhouette, contemplating Tara from above. *Strategia del ragno* (dir. Bernardo Bertolucci, Radiotelevisione Italiana, 1970).

In this tower scene, the director alludes possibly to the reference to the tower at the beginning of Borges's short story. A paratextual quote, a passage from the Yeats poem "The Tower," elaborates on the idea of man's contingency and powerlessness: "all men are dancers and their tread / goes to the barbarous clangour of a gong" (*OC* 1: 496). Man is nothing but a marionette, moved according to the rhythm of a brutal gong. There is also a tower mentioned in the text. The burning circular tower in Kilpatrick's home town is interpreted as a negative omen, foreshadowing his death. In the filmic variation, Bertolucci presents the protagonist, sentenced to death, as a silhouette on a tower; he is moving and gesticulating in front of a colored, three-dimensional entity, which is the town of Tara. Athos Sr.'s hope to regain dominance over the space through the geographical exposure is illusionary. The mirror and the tower, in relation to the act of a theatrical staging, are also key elements in a critical discourse Bertolucci valued greatly. In his study of the formation of the ego, especially during the early stage of individual development and the child's self-recognition and positioning in a social context, Jacques Lacan analyzes the roles of the mirror and the tower:

> I… regard the function of the mirror-stage as a particular case of the function of the *imago*, which is to establish a relation between the organism and its reality. … The *mirror stage* is a drama […] which manufactures for the subject, caught up in the lure of spatial identification, the succession of phantasies [*sic*] that extends from a fragmented body-image to a form of its totality. … Correlatively, the formation of the *I* is symbolized in dreams by a fortress… where the subject flounders in quest of the lofty, remote, inner castle. (4–5)

In this regard, the character's relation to mirrors and the tower, shown in the film, can be interpreted as an allusion to Athos Sr.'s mental "regression" from the social to the pre-mirror stadium, from the powerful spokesman and social performer to a mere black silhouette, shown without any connection to the space. On top of the tower, he turns into a shadow, similar to the marionette in Yeats's poem, foreshadowing his own death.

Borges and Bertolucci, each in his medium, present a plurality of puzzling stages that are juxtaposed, reflected, or mixed into each other. Their artistic elaborations are highly self-reflexive. In the text and the film, the work of art is made and unmade before the eyes of the readers and viewers. This metanarrative theme is, among others, conveyed by the spatial settings: Borges initially evokes a vague, changeable place. The plot might be deferred and repeated ("tal vez") at another site, in another timeframe. Similar to a challenging of the temporal logics, the story deconstructs a spatial hierarchy and separation such as the binary opposition of a stage and an audience. Space, like time, constitutes a shifting frame of reference for the narrator Ryan, who, at the end, wonders if he himself is an actor in a plot of changing stages, foreseen by an absent and omniscient stage director.

Both Borges's and Bertolucci's fictions, according to Bolongaro, focus "on the problem of history and its representation, as well as on the role of intertextuality in fiction/film making" (74). Concurring with Bolongaro, I interpret the film as a much more clearly political commentary on strategies of mythologizing (the hero of the Italian anti-Fascist Resistance) than the short story, although I would not go so far as to state that "Borges' closure of the narrative circle is a surrender to a metaphysical fantasy… [and that] one of the many merits of Bertolucci's film is the rejection of [Borges'] mesmerizing metaphysics" (88). Precisely because Borges's narrator focuses to such a degree on the difficulty of situatedness of the plots and spatial facts, he highlights the specificity of each of the strategies of fictionalization and the need to carefully study them individually and in comparison and not present them as mere sequences of instances in a chain of repetitions without any difference.

The *atopos* in Borges's and Bertolucci's intermedial pair is much more developed than in "Hombre de la esquina rosada." While Borges and Picazo start to challenge a fixed spatiality with, for instance, the description and presentation of entirely black sites, in "Tema del traidor y del héroe" and *Strategia del ragno*, the theme of a negative space that is characterized as a space of an "absence du lui à lui-même" (Augé 108), is much more thoroughly developed and presented through multiple technical and thematic elements. In his film, Bertolucci elaborates on this blurring of clear spatial differentiations and, metapoetically, on the cinematographic medium's techniques and effects of staging (or, as the French language significantly describes it, as a *mise en scène*). The train entering the station reminds one of the birth of cinema and, figuratively, introduces the viewers to the filmic stage. Less abstract than Borges's text, the film by the Italian director centers on a concise place. Tara is present as a toponym, a repeatedly filmed graphic sign in the surroundings, and a three-dimensional setting. With its theater, the Renaissance archways, the town is a carefully arranged stage for Athos Jr.'s investigation, a site of inertia, a remembrance set in stone, evoking over and over again the hero's acts. Through its various emulations, framing devices, and reflecting mirrors, it becomes an inscrutable entity for Athos Jr., who feels entrapped in the confined microcosm of disconcerting, plural, and deferred visions. Like his father thirty years earlier, he is increasingly caught in the web of Tara. Athos Sr. was reduced to a black gesticulating silhouette in front of the town's panorama, reminiscent of the shell of an insect in a spider's web. The son is petrified and immobilized, gazing at the railroad tracks that are overgrown with weeds, reminiscent of an insect bitten by a spider, staring at the threads of the inescapable net.

The space in Borges's and Bertolucci's plot or web (the Spanish and Italian word *trama* refers both to a narrative plot or theme and to an interweavement of threads such as a spider's web) is changeable, unstable, and therefore disconcerting. Space for Ryan and for Athos Jr. reflects a staging according to a latent screenplay. The characters face deferrals and deconstructions of formerly homogeneous surroundings. The more they investigate, the more they are trapped in an inescapable net of fiction.

Chapter Three

Screening the Void

Julio Cortázar's "Cartas de mamá," and Manuel Antin's and Miguel Picazo's Filmic Translations

In 1946 Julio Cortázar published his first work of fiction in a literary magazine, whose editor was none other than Jorge Luis Borges, by then the most influential writer of short prose in Argentina. As Jaime Alazraki points out, like any other writer of the genre in the 1940s and 50s, Cortázar had to establish his place in relation to Borges:

> Cortázar comenzó a escribir sus primeros cuentos dentro de un medio en que el magisterio de Borges era el eje de la vida literaria en Buenos Aires, verdadero Minotauro de las letras porteñas: todos los caminos iban a dar al centro de ese laberinto intelectual que el autor de *Ficciones* había tejido desde los años veinte con el rigor y la paciencia dedálica de un arquitecto. (57)

Cortázar was an avid reader and prolific critic of fiction of the nineteenth and the beginning of the twentieth centuries.[1] Like many of his compatriots, Cortázar was fascinated by Borges's textual creations of infinite libraries, his re-elaborations of philosophical and theological arguments and of literary and mythical themes. But Cortázar's writing is strikingly different from that of Borges. The former does not build his texts on existing narratives, arguments, and epistemes like the author of *Ficciones.*[2] Again in Alazraki's words, "si Borges es un frecuentador de mapas, Cortázar es un explorador de regiones no cartografiadas" (142). Many of Cortázar's short texts and novels are based on descriptions of everyday situations: A man is on the Parisian metro, an amateur photographer is taking some random snapshots, a man is just about to take off his sweater in his bedroom. But gradually these accounts of daily occurrences become transformed. The metro stations are taken over by a party of pale beings; the lonely city dweller feels that the act of having taken the photograph has prevented a crime; the man with his face buried in the fluffy texture of the sweater and his arms twisted as if in a straitjacket, makes a move toward the open window and experiences a fatal fall. Cortázar's short stories and novels echo Louis Aragon's poetology of the "merveilleux quotidien," elaborated in *Le paysan de Paris* (*Paris Peasant*).[3] As in Aragon, Cortázar's protagonists discover a marvelous otherness within the daily grind. For both authors the descriptions of different layers of reality lead toward a poetics that does away with the dualistic conceptions of the ordinary, artless life versus a refined, consciously formed work of art. In a letter to Manuel Antin, Cortázar elaborates on the role of the marvelous in the quotidian. When describing Luis Buñuel's film *El ángel exterminador* (*The Exterminating Angel*), he explains: "[Es] una película alucinante y, en el fondo, absolutamente fantástica, en el sentido que yo le doy a lo fantástico, es decir lo inmediatamente cotidiano visto bajo una luz de revelación" (Cortázar, *Cartas 1937–1963* 495–96). The intrusion of a slightly estranged element into an ordinary and common space, a sudden thought, gesture, reaction, or a point of view, opens up the horizon of the marvelous.[4]

Another poetological basis in Cortázar's writings, which clearly distinguishes him from his predecessor Borges, is the importance of the visual. Many of Cortázar's texts elaborate on visual perception, on the juxtaposition and overlapping of images, and more generally on the role of the human eye in making sense of the world. His characters perceive seemingly unimportant situations with extraordinary acuteness. An example is the minute description of a sugar cube that falls onto the dark floor in a café in *Rayuela* (*Hopscotch*) [1963]. For the protagonist, the image of the white cube on the black surface provokes a metaphysical meditation on the human condition, followed by a frantic search for the fallen piece amid the table legs and shoes of the other customers.

Cortázar's quest for literary equivalents of visual snapshots was much in vogue during the 1950s and 60s in his then residence, Paris. In 1962, Alain Robbe-Grillet, the self-proclaimed leader of the French *Nouveau Roman* movement, published a book with the significant title *Instantanés* (*Snapshots*).[5] The word *instantané*, which can be translated into English with the adjective "instantaneous" or with the noun "snapshot," alludes to the technique of rapid visual recording. Such a quick shot, free from all premeditation, might expose unusual perspectives to the viewer and allow the broadening of perception. A paragraph from Cortázar's early novel *Los premios* (*The Winners*) [1960] exemplifies such a literary analogy of a photographic snapshot. In the text, one of the characters, while inattentively looking out of his cabin on a ship, catches sight of another passenger who is walking by: "Exactamente en el marco de la puerta, se recortó la imagen de perfil de Carlos López, que en ese momento levantaba la pierna derecha para dar otro paso. Su brusca aparición le dio a Raúl la impresión de una de esas instantáneas de un caballo en movimiento" (60). The mention of the image of a horse in motion alludes to one of the first photographic sequences ever made, the series of a galloping horse. This series of early photographic instants from 1877, commissioned by Leland Stanford, proved that, at a certain moment, none of the horse's hooves touched the ground. As Benjamin would later point out in his essay on art in the age of mechanical reproduction, the new medium had revealed a fact the human eye was unable to capture. Many of Cortázar's writings elaborate on new modes of perception, similar to the broadening of human perception through the photographic technique.

In Cortázar's works, the *atopos* appears through the combination of the literary "instantanés" and the verbal discoveries of the everyday marvel. These active non-spaces again dissolve the notion of a stable background. As in Borges's and Sábato's texts, Cortázar's literary sites have a major impact on the characters and the development of the narration. He often presents dual or triple settings that mesh in the characters' practices of space, such as in the short stories "Lejana. Diario de Alina Reyes" ("The Distances") (*Bestiario/Bestiary*) [1951], "Axolotl" (*idem*) or "La noche boca arriba" ("The Night Face Up") (both from *Final del juego/The End of the Game*) [1956]. In these short stories, the characters are forced to interact with fantastic spaces of extreme instability. For instance, the protagonist of "Axolotl" fluidly changes positions and worldviews; he is at one point outside an aquarium in the Parisian *Jardin des Plantes*, and at another point on the other side of the half inch of glass, in the water, transformed into an axolotl (Moran 4; Sánchez 38–40). Like many other characters, he is caught in an ambiguous in-between space. For Saúl Yurkiévich, in his introduction to Cortázar's collected works, this specific spatiality is the result of the author's literary optics: "Los cuentos de Cortázar nacen de una visión desplazada, fuera de foco, o visión 'intersticial'… de estar entre, no por encima, ni por detrás sino entre" (*OC* 1: 16–17). *Rayuela* exemplifies such an in-between space, now built on melancholy. On the one hand, the characters come upon present places that appear unreal, and, on the other hand, they come into imagined spaces that nevertheless possess a haunting reality. The traveler Oliveira, together with his friend and alter ego, the sedentary Traveler, encounters and moreover constructs microcosms of vagueness and spatial oscillation. For example, they build a precarious bridge made out of a wooden plank over the inner courtyard between their apartments in Buenos Aires and create three-dimensional spatial models from yarn in different rooms and over various floors of a mental hospital. In Paris, Oliveira and his lover, Maga, play games of juxtaposing worlds through words and discover that "dos mundos distantes, ajenos, casi siempre inconciliables, entran en nuestras palabras" (ch. 138, *OC* 3: 593). Cortázar does not position a duality of spaces for the readers to select one and return to the safe harbor of binary oppositions. On the contrary, the irreconcilable sites are overlapping, merging, and thus creating a new space of contiguity. Carlos Alonso, in "To Burn Like This without Surcease," explains that "the dynamics ruling Cortázar's works [are] not built on the dissolution of opposition by effecting a movement from one pole to the other, but rather on the displacement away from the dichotomy itself to a third 'position' that defines a space in which those categories are suspended or rendered ineffectual" (in *Julio Cortázar—New Readings* 10). What is described, then, is not a toponym, such as "Buenos Aires" or "Paris," but a third, interstitial, and dynamic site of instantaneity.

In *Buenos Aires, Buenos Aires* (*idem*) [1968], the essay for a collection of photos of the Argentinean capital, Cortázar devises distance within closeness. After accompanying two photographers to his former home town, he writes the text when he is back in France, with Paris serving as the spatial counterpoint to the Argentinean capital.[6] The return goes hand in hand with an irrecoverable alienation, presented in a fragmentary narrative fashion: "Así, el familiar ha llegado hasta otra esquina… extrañeza… ahora que vuelve a andar en estas imágenes que pasan por sus dedos mientras lo que queda en él… del joven hombre viejo… enajenación" (23). While *Rayuela* presents collages and oscillations between sites of a "here" that is not necessarily joined with a "now" opposed to a "there" that does not necessarily go with a "then" and while *Buenos Aires, Buenos Aires* describes a "here" that contains in itself an alienating "not here," the space-fiction in the later novel *62. Modelo para armar* (*62. A Model Kit*) [1968] is even more extreme. The three cities that provide the background for the narration are merging. As if Paris, London, and Vienna were laid on top on each other, the encounters and situations take place in the simultaneity of interconnected and interchangeable spaces. By means of an analogy with photography, the description parallels the photographic technique of fading images, which projects several photos on one single surface.[7] One of the "decentered" characters of the novel, an interpreter who is traveling to and fro between countries and languages, meditates about the City (at the beginning written with a capital letter, to distinguish this space from cities of common experiences): "La Ciudad… podía darse en París, en una cervecería de Oslo, a alguno de nosotros le había ocurrido pasar de la ciudad a una cama de Barcelona, a menos que no fuera lo contrario. La ciudad no se explicaba, era; había emergido alguna vez en las conversaciones" (*OC* 3: 646). The ghostlike *non-lieu* in *62. Modelo para armar* has no fixed boundaries. As the title suggests, it has to be created and modeled both by the characters and by the readers.

Besides describing figures that change in oscillating places, Cortázar often portrays moved objects in space, such as letters. A letter, a small, fragile element of exceptional mobility, connects different times and places; yet it also highlights the spatio-temporal gaps, since it is written in a past and is sent to a future. In "Carta a una señorita en París" ("Letter to a Young Lady in Paris," *Bestiario*) a man in Buenos Aires writes to the owner of his apartment in Paris (Cortázar wrote this text when he was still living in Buenos Aires). The short story "Cartas de mamá" ("Letters from Mama," *Las armas secretas, The Secret Weapons*), which also mentions the object of the letter in its title, was published in Buenos Aires in 1959, after Cortázar had moved to France. In contrast to "Carta a una señorita en París," "Cartas de mamá" is written from the vantage point of an Argentinean who has immigrated to the French capital and receives letters from his mother back in Argentina.

Luis, the protagonist of the short story, lives in a seemingly secure space. He appears to enjoy a harmonious life with his wife and to be satisfied with his job. However, this idyll is only illusory. He feels perpetually uneasy, as he is confronted by a plurality of past and present sites. The letters from his mother become mental attacks on his life and the space he inhabits. In the first sentence of the text, Luis compares his life in Paris with the situation of a prisoner released on parole: "Muy bien hubiera podido llamarse libertad condicional" (*OC* 1: 251). When he sees the stamp with the head of José de San Martín, he realizes that he is about to "franquear el puente" (*OC* 1: 251) to the city of his past. The name and the image remind him of

> San Martín, Rivadavia, pero esos nombres eran también imágenes de calles y cosas; Rivadavia a seis mil quinientos, el caserón de Flores, mamá, el café de San Martín y Corrientes, donde lo esperaban a veces los amigos, donde el mazagrán tenía un leve gusto a aceite de ricino. Con el sobre en la mano, después del *Merci bien, madame Durand,* salir a la calle no era ya lo mismo. (*OC* 1: 251)

The small object in his hands radically alters Luis's perception of his usual surroundings and conjures up past spaces, situations, and even flavors. The impact of the letter is almost like a physical blow: "Cada carta de mamá… cambiaba de golpe la vida de Luis, lo devolvía al pasado como un duro rebote de pelota" (*OC* 1: 251). As a result, the images and emotions of the past cloud his perception of the present. After having been mentally thrown back to Buenos Aires, Luis is unable to perceive his actual life-world. Sitting in the bus, on his way to work, as he is staring out the window, he sees opaque surroundings: "Cada… carta insinuaba… que su nueva vida recortada con feroces golpes de tijera en la madeja de lana… su libertad duramente conquistada… se borraba como el fondo de las calles mientras el autobús corría por la rue de Richelieu" (*OC* 1: 251). Luis has fought arduously for his new life in Paris. But upon receiving the letter he has the impression that his present life is erased just as the three-dimensional space around him begins to blur.

A letter incorporates an irretrievable past (the past presence of the sender) that is carried to an equally absent future (the future presence of the receiver). The message moves through an interstitial space with uncertain characteristics. Luis seems to share some of its characteristics: Not only has he become estranged from his presence in Paris, in addition, he is unable to return entirely to the spatio-temporal past. The letter is also the carrier of other absences. According to Jacques Derrida, the written name points toward a paradoxical, self-effacing presence:

> Le nom ne soit ce qui s'efface devant ce qu'il nomme, et alors "il faut le nom" voudrait dire que le nom fait défaut. *Arrivant* alors à *s'effacer,* il *sera sauf lui-même* [...] Donner un nom, est-ce encore donner? ... On peut en douter, dès lors que non seulement le nom n'est rien, en tout cas n'est pas la "chose" qu'il nomme, pas le "nommable" ou le renommé, mais risque aussi d'enchaîner, d'asservir ou d'engager l'autre, de lier l'appelé, de l'appeler à répondre, avant même toute décision ou toute délibération, avant même toute liberté. (*Sauf le nom* 80, 112; emphasis in original)

The name of the mother, similar to the fragile letter itself, expresses an absence that possesses a restrictive power over its receiver. In the case of the message that Luis receives, this absence is even intensified, since Mamá writes about her other son Nico, who had died two years before. However, she mentions Nico's name as if he were still alive. This sudden intrusion shocks Luis, who had not brought up his brother's name since Nico's death, just as his wife and mother had not. "La repentina mención de su nombre... era casi un escándalo... el nombre de Nico apareci[ó] de golpe en una frase, con la N larga y temblorosa, la o con una cola torcida... Un punto apenas marcado con la débil tinta azul comprada en el almacén del barrio... 'Esta mañana Nico preguntó por ustedes'" (*OC* 1: 254). The name conjures the image of Luis's dead brother. The graphical representation of the word *Nico* even projects some of his characteristics onto the paper. The letter *N* is large and thin, written possibly by a hand that did not hold the pen very firmly. The *o* is ended by a strange line and the dot on the *i* is scarcely visible. Even before Luis describes Nico, the letters that are constitutive of the brother's name figuratively convey the idea of a trembling and unhappy body.[8] Cortázar's Nico, a graphical representation and a reminiscence of times past, wanders through the mother's textual universe and makes his way into his brother's life.

Nico had been Laura's fiancé until Luis started a secret affair with her, when Nico fell ill with tuberculosis. After Nico's death, Luis and Laura married and moved to Paris to escape the resentment of the family and just as much, to flee their own feelings of guilt and shame. In order to build a new life, both spouses had tried to silence the past, particularly those aspects of it that were related to Nico. Through her letters, showing probably the first signs of a memory defect, Mamá now names the long-silenced cause of the couple's present trauma.

Besides the letters and names, silence is a third motif in "Cartas de mamá" that circumscribes the *atopos* of an absence in a present space-time. Luis and Laura had agreed—silently—never to mention the name of the brother. In the beginning, this silencing had been a relief for Luis. Later, he had attempted repeatedly to break the taboo, but Laura would resist. By being hidden obstinately, the name had turned into a perpetual presence:

> Laura seguía sin nombrarlo, y él [Luis]… sabiendo que en el fondo ese silencio lo agraviaba por lo que tenía de reproche, de arrepentimiento, de algo que empezaba a parecerse a la traición… Un lento territorio prohibido se había ido formando poco a poco en su lenguaje, aislándolos de Nico, envolviendo su nombre y su recuerdo en un algodón manchado y pegajoso. Y del otro lado, mamá hacía lo mismo, confabulaba inexplicablemente en el silencio… [Era un] pacto involuntario de silencio en que los dos se desunían poco a poco. (*OC* 1: 257)

After interrupting the situation of a traumatic amnesia with the note that the brother has asked about the couple, in her next letter, Mamá announces that Nico is planning to travel to Europe. While reading this letter, still on the bus, Luis is further estranged from his surroundings: "De calle en calle fue sintiendo como le costaba situarse en el presente" (*OC* 1: 260). This violent breaking of the entrenched silence brings hurt to Luis, but also offers him new insights. He becomes aware of Laura's emotional distance and the existence of a "prohibited territory" that has grown between them. One night, Laura wakes up screaming from her nightmares, but will not tell her husband about them. Luis is convinced that she had been dreaming about her former fiancé and the house on Suipacha Street. Laura's dreams conjure up the characters and spaces from the past, both for herself and for her husband, who, because of his wife's silence, in turn begins to imagine the scenes she might have created and seen in her dreams.

Eventually, Mamá sends a third letter with detailed information on Nico's arrival in Paris. Luis knows that, all logic notwithstanding, Laura will be waiting for Nico at the train station. On the day of the announced arrival of the dead brother, he follows her and observes her waiting for the ghost of her former lover—to no avail. Her face has the same expression as when she wakes up from a nightmare. When Luis returns home in the evening, she pretends that she has not left the apartment for the whole day. He does not comment on the lie. Yet, the territory of silence between the spouses has expanded further. Nico has taken possession of the mute, interstitial space between them.

> La mentira de Laura ya no importaba, una más entre tantos besos ajenos, tantos silencios donde todo era Nico, donde no había nada en ella o en él que no fuera Nico. ¿Por qué no poner un tercer cubierto en la mesa? … Quizás [Nico] estaba en la otra habitación, o se había instalado ya donde siempre había sido el amo, en el territorio blanco y tibio de las sábanas al que tantas veces había acudido en los sueños de Laura… Sentía la casa como un puño que se fuera apretando. Todo era más estrecho, más sofocante. (*OC* 1: 268–69)

Luis's claustrophobic impression is increased when he recalls Mamá's spacious house in Buenos Aires. He decides to speak to his wife about Nico (although he avoids pronouncing the brother's name) as if the brother had actually come to visit them. After telling Laura that "he" (Nico) does not look very healthy, she calmly replies: "Un poco. Uno va cambiando…" (*OC* 1: 269). At the end, Nico has become the only topic of conversation, albeit without mentioning his name directly. The "forbidden territory" of the dead takes over the Parisian apartment, which had been created as a space of freedom in contrast to the guilt-infested house in Buenos Aires. Nico, conjured up by the mother's letters and the couple's silence, based on the suffocating feelings of fault that ties them together, becomes the void, untouchable, and invisible center of their relationship.

"Cartas de mamá" presents juxtapositions and the merging of places. It also describes Luis's inability to grasp a place in its entirety, and consequently to situate himself in the surrounding space. He has the impression that his present life and vicinity are dissolving. But the remembrance of the city of his past remains equally indistinct and intangible. Carlos Alonso elaborates on the topic of the interstitial space in Cortázar's writing and on its aesthetic and epistemological implications:

> Perhaps Cortázar's search for a way out of the epistemological dichotomies of Western knowledge may not represent the author's debt to surrealism or paraphysics, as is commonly held, but rather a coeval and sui generic exploration of issues that preoccupied thinkers such as Derrida, Lacan, Serres, and several others. Timothy Reiss has said, for instance, that… the principal "elements" of Derridean discourse: "margin," "supplement," "différence," "deferral," "athesis" and so on can all be subsumed under a paradigm of "between" (*entre*)… it is as though this discourse wished to expand the "space" of the limits themselves… "Space" is of course the wrong term. "Between" is a better indication of the attempt. (14)

Cortázar's short story is exemplary for this quest for and creation of sites of the in-between that allow for new insights beyond traditional epistemological and narrative limits. This "in-betweenness" of the spaces of absence in "Cartas de mamá" proves to be inspirational for visual artists.

Only three years after the publication of the short story, the Argentinean director Manuel Antin produced *La cifra impar* (The Odd Number, 1962). In 1978, the Spanish director Miguel Picazo shot the homonymous *Cartas de mamá*. The fortunate existence of two filmic versions of Cortázar's short story allows me to embark on a comparative, intermedial study of their respective third spaces of absence, first between the text and the films and second, between both films. *La cifra impar* is Antin's first film.[9] It is also the first in a long list of adaptations of Cortázar's short stories.[10] The black-and-white film begins with darkness. After a few seconds, the screen shows a rectangular ray of light, then the camera moves to the portrait of a young woman next to it, and finally, the face of an old woman in the middle of the illuminated area. The faces of the portrait and the old woman are about the same size (see fig. 3.1). This puzzling initial situation is resolved when the scene is illuminated entirely: The camera is located inside a wardrobe and films the entering light. The old woman standing outside the wardrobe is captured in the process of opening the doors of this black box containing the camera. In turn, the image of the painting is seen reflected in a mirror, facing the doors of the wardrobe. Since the actual painting is leaned against the back of the wardrobe, next to the camera, its reflection disappears as the doors are opened completely. Right from the beginning, the projected spaces in *La cifra impar* are inserted into each other. The viewers

Fig 3.1. Still with "Mamá," juxtaponed with a painting of Laura from the beginning of *La cifra impar* (dir. Manuel Antin, Norma Vigo, 1962). Reproduced with permission of the director, Universidad del Cinema, Buenos Aires, Argentina.

see several alternations of total darkness and light, juxtapositions of similar motifs in front of moving backgrounds as well as reflections in a mirror.

The woman slowly leaves the room and descends the stairs with her hand on the banister. She walks to an old bureau while a clock strikes the hour. The camera focuses on two framed photographs on the bureau, the bigger one showing a man (Nico), the smaller one showing a couple (Laura and Luis). The woman sits down and starts to write a letter. Her hand and the letter are filmed through a mirror, which is placed on the back side of the bureau. While the pen moves over the paper with screeching noises, her voice off scene narrates: "El Boby está bien… Esta mañana, Nico preguntó por ustedes." During the opening credits, for about a minute, the camera shows her face, scarcely moving, in front of an entirely dark background. The beginning of the film presents the mother's existence as characterized by repetitions, remembrances, and reflections. Then the scene changes and shows a modern entrance door and a hand slipping a letter under this door. In the following shot, the camera is inside a modern apartment, suggesting that the letter, just like the film camera, entered through the door. A man (Luis) picks the letter up from the floor. While he opens the envelope, a female voice (Laura's) asks if he received any important mail, which he quickly denies. The following scene shows Laura standing in front of a mirror. Next, Luis is seen placing the letter in his jacket, before he opens the locks of the apartment door, ready to leave for work. "Tantas cerraduras," he notes slightly annoyed. "¿De quién tenés miedo? Ladrones no hay. Y los fantasmas se filtran." After he has left the apartment, Laura approaches the door, repeats to herself "se filtran," picks up a remaining piece of the letter from the floor, and stares at it for several seconds. She returns to the mirror, observes her image, and goes to a bureau (similar to Mamá's), which displays a photograph of Luis's mother on top of it (just as Mamá had photographs of her sons and Laura on her desk). She opens the piece of furniture and takes out a bundle of letters. While she holds them in her hand, the mother's voice continues: "Estoy bastante bien… Aquí hubo revolución. Unos tanques. Me enteré por la radio… A veces no entiendo la letra de Laura. Deberías de escribirme vos." While Mamá's voice continues, the screen shows both spouses in their Parisian surroundings, Laura in front of the mirrors with the letters and Luis on the way to his office.

The mirrors, together with the letter, the photographs, and the portrait of Laura, introduce an *atopos* of a disconcerting multiplicity of space-times. The non-space in Antin's film is deceiving because it entraps its inhabitants in a multitude of reflections that elude any reliable remembrance and hence ascertainment of the present self. The objects may serve as supplements of certain moments that maybe never were. In "The Memory of Pictures: Roland Barthes and Augustine on Photography," Anselm Haverkamp remarks accordingly:

> The universal success of the picture-taking, memory-storing activity has, in the manner of a supplement (the truest supplement, perhaps, of our life-world), supplanted what it is supposed to subserve, memory as well as its content, "life." It is no surprise… that the photograph as the most real representation of what there is seems to be most congenial to serve the remembrance of things past and to make present in a supplementary

> way what maybe never was (except for the picture taken...) (258)

Many of the secondary representations in *La cifra impar* are supplements in Haverkamp's sense of the concept. These mirrors, images, paintings, and letters create an atmosphere of multiple times and spaces—remembered, projected, and imagined—that often leave no place for Laura's and Luis's experience of the present. Besides the focus on these objects, Antin relies on two cinematographic techniques to convey multiple time-spaces: the flashbacks and flash-forwards that are interwoven in the filmic narration and the voices off-screen that accompany the characters in locations that are often dissociated from the speech contexts.

The film has a large number of flashbacks and flash-forwards.[11] Several of the settings in *La cifra impar* that are placed next to each other via flashbacks and flash-forwards contain common elements. An example of this is the showing of beds that appear in successive scenes. In a sequence of about twenty seconds the screen first portrays Nico, lying on his bed, while his mother is bringing him his medicine. This shot is followed by a scene with Laura and Luis in a bed, possibly in a hotel room, after having slept with each other. Laura suddenly says that for her, Nico is already a dead man who is still alive. (This second shot is possibly no flashback or flash-forward, but takes place simultaneously with the first shot.) In a third shot (a flash-forward with relation to the preceding scenes of the sequence), the screen shows the marital bed in Laura's and Luis's apartment in Paris. In this image, the spouses are both in bed, with their backs turned against each other, pretending to sleep so as to avoid corporeal contact. The presence of the same object in these different shots conveys the idea that, beyond their apparent heterogeneity, they belong together. The juxtaposition of these sequences generates, not always a narrative succession, but a mood of haunting guilt.[12]

The frequency of flashbacks and flash-forwards increases toward the end of the film, as Nico's bodiless presence imposes itself more and more on the spouses. In one of the final sequences, the characters engage in the following dialogue:

> Laura: Sufrió... Sufrió.
> Luis: ¿Querés decir que entre vos y yo, lo hicimos sufrir?
> Laura: Quiero decir más... entre vos y yo lo hemos matado.

Luis: Es inútil tratar de convencernos que él haya muerto. Sigue vivo... Dejemos este juego.

During this short dialogue, starting in a park in Paris, the film presents various other settings (Nico in the kitchen in the house in Buenos Aires, then in his room, painting Laura's portrait, followed by several shots from Laura's and Luis's life in Paris). What started out as a flashback from the present in Paris to the past in Buenos Aires turns into a flash-forward from the present in Buenos Aires to the future in Paris, perhaps imagined by the spouses or by Nico. Thus, the flashbacks and flash-forwards overlap and are inserted one into another. In order to refer to a preceding or a subsequent action, there has to be a clearly defined present instance. Antin, however, challenges the idea of a single present within a linear filmic narrative by interlocking a large number of shots that belong to different spatio-temporal frames. Instead of a chronological narration, the film shows a juxtaposition of "instantanés." If the supposed flashback in relation to a present moment in the narration is itself the frame for another spatio-temporal setting, which, in turn, is cut off by another flashback or flash-forward, the characters' (and the audience's) certainty about a precise present moment in relation to the past and to the future, fades. In such a vertiginous interweavement and proliferation of visual images the notion of reliable space-time blurs. Antin's atmospheric setting is similar to a stream of consciousness where every mental image can be compared to a knot in a net of "presences."

Besides the visual juxtapositions and entanglements, Antin also draws on the sound track to suggest the presence of the dead and invisible man. This is accomplished by means of a refined use of voices off-screen. For Laura and Luis, Mamá's voice is omnipresent. Laura hears her speak while doing housework, when she is walking through Paris, and even in her dreams. Similarly, Luis cannot escape Mamá's mournful voice while he goes about his daily work. The voice of the (physically) absent mother only reinforces a present silence. An example of this silencing is a scene at Luis's work, when his colleague asks him if he feels all right. Luis replies that everything is fine. With his mouth shut, his voice conveys his inner monologue: "Lo que me pasa es … Nico … Nico es mi hermano. Nunca hablo de él. Sobre todo no con Laura … Es como un rebote… Todo eso… muy bien pudiera llamarse libertad condicional…" In many scenes of *La cifra impar*, the human voice, that medium traditionally associated with pure presence, refers to absence. Antin uses a simple technical fact of film to reach this effect: The sound track and the film spool do not correspond. The speakers and their voices are not shown and played simultaneously. Mamá's voice, from a "nowhere" place of the past, acquires a traumatizing presence for Laura and Luis. Over and over again, in different contexts, this voice is repeating the same sentence with the fatal *lapsus linguae*: "Esta mañana Nico preguntó por ustedes." The demonstrative pronoun with its concise temporal qualification cannot be related to any actual moment, neither in Laura's and Luis's nor in Mamá's life-world. "This morning" alludes to an impossible presence, since it could refer to any morning before or after Nico's death. The sentence in itself with its almost spellbinding rhythm (the accents on the vowels are in an alternating binary and tertiary structure "**é**st**a** (2) / m**a**ñ**a**n**a** (3) / N**i**c**o** (2) / pr**e**g**u**nt**ó** (3) / p**o**r [u]st**e**d**e**s (3)") contributes to a liminal atmosphere outside ordinary time and space.

Many of the sentences that are uttered by mere bodiless voices are repeated or reiterated in slightly modified ways. The motif of repetition and variation is another element that breaks the linear progression and intensifies the traumatizing atmosphere of a haunting past enmeshed with a blurred presence. An example is the question, together with its variations, about the characters' states of mind. When Luis's colleague asks him in French "Qu'est-ce qui te passe?" he quickly replies "rien," before his voice continues in Spanish: "lo que me pasa es… Nico." Laura uses the same verb, when she asks Nico, back in Buenos Aires: "Pregúntame lo que me pasa." He then replies, again using the same verb: "No debería de pasarte nada." In a later scene, after having met Luis, Laura's voice narrates: "Soy como todos. Nunca me pasa nada. Y de repente me pasa algo." In Paris, while she is staring at her image in the mirror, Luis asks her "¿Laura, qué te pasa?" whereupon she answers: "Nada. ¿Qué puede pasarme?" In a later scene, again facing a mirror, her voice meditates: "No pasa nada. ¿Ha pasado algo en París? La vida es sorprendentemente fácil acá." Then she remembers a situation back in Buenos Aires, when Nico took her home after the dancing party at which she met his brother. Jealously, he asked: "¿Se puede saber lo que te pasa?" And again, she replied "Nada." The excessive repetition of a similar question and answer creates an atmosphere of echo and of deferral, both backward and forward. The insistence on nothingness underscores the perceived lack of reliable chrono-spatiological grounding. Through repetitions in time and the echoing in space of certain expressions, Antin creates an atmospheric space, similar to Cortázar's.

In his analysis of *La cifra impar*, David Oubiña describes the technique of sharp cuttings and juxtapositions of various shots as a visual analogue to the literary device of indirect free speech. He notes: "Antin construye una especie de discurso indirecto libre audiovisual… Dota a las imágenes de una naturaleza ambigua… Reemplaza la invisibilidad del corte por una sinuosa fluidez de fragmentos" (15). In a text, the technique of free indirect speech consists of the presentation of an enunciation that cannot be related unambiguously to a speaking instance. This means of expression obliges the readers to actively assign an enunciation to an intradiegetic or extradiegetic speaker. Thus, it "imposes an alienating uncertainty of judgment" (Jauß 203; my translation). I agree with Oubiña that in Antin's adaptation the camera's point of view, the filmic equivalent of the narrator in a literary work, is highly ambiguous. The audience does not know for certain which character observes or imagines the scenes that are shown on the screen. Some shots (most of them presenting empty spaces) could be moments remembered by Luis or by Laura; they could also be experiences attributed to Nico or Mamá. For instance, the shot of the couple seen through bars, shown several times over the course of the film, could be Mamá's view from inside the house in Buenos Aires, when she is waiting for her sons to return home (see fig. 3.2). It could also be Laura's memory of a day in the garden, when she was looking through the fence, as she was confessing to her fiancé Nico that there was something missing in her life. The shot might also be a symbolic image of Luis's perception of his present life in Paris, where he feels trapped like in the prison cell of the traumatic past, built around the house with the railing on Suipacha Street, which reminds him of the bars of a cage in a Parisian park. The places are presented without a specific relation to any of the characters. For this reason, I interpret many sites in *La cifra impar* as shared past, present, or future spaces of each of the characters. Mamá's visual imagination of a street corner in Paris might be the site of Laura's actual experience. Luis's remembrance of a scene with Nico getting off a train might as well be the visualization of one of Laura's nightmares. Many situations are lived, dreamed, remembered, or imagined alternatively by any one

Fig. 3.2. Luis and Laura, filmed through the barren gate. *La cifra impar* (dir. Manuel Antin, Norma Vigo, 1962). Reproduced with permission of the director, Universidad del Cinema, Buenos Aires, Argentina.

of the four characters. Thus, the settings, instead of being sites of interaction among individuals, are the conjunction of individual traumata that are blended into each other in a presence of a collective remembrance.

While at the beginning of the film, Mamá writes a letter to her son in Paris, in its final scene, Luis is writing a letter to her. By now, he has adapted himself to Mamá's and Laura's traumatic perceptions of Nico's continuous presence. Nico, the obstinate specter from Buenos Aires, has arrived in Paris, just as Mamá had announced and just as Laura had sensed all the time. Luis's voice provides an account of the content of his letter: "Mamá. Nico llegó… Estaba en todas partes. Está en todas partes… Nico está… siempre estuvo… Tan en todas partes. ¿Por qué nos hizo eso, mamá?" The grammatical subject of the last sentence is ambiguous (provided that Luis addresses his mother with the formal "usted"). Luis may be accusing either Nico or Mamá of having destroyed his and Laura's life in Paris. In this regard, the end of the film is even more ambiguous than the final sentences of the short story. The effect of Nico's or Mamá's acts, on the contrary, is far from ambiguous. Luis has no doubt about the brother's invisible presence between

Laura and himself. The odd number, to which the title of the film alludes, has filled the interstice between the two lovers. The ghost, mentioned by Laura and Luis at the beginning of the film, has come to occupy all of the couple's shared spaces. Nico's invisible and silenced presence (the spouses return to not mentioning his name at the end of the film, even when they talk about him) has taken over and rearranged their space. His territory of control over the traumatized brother and the former fiancée has expanded. The word *Nico*, this verbal remnant of a dead man that is expanding in space through the sound waves, which is also reproduced on a piece of paper, ready to be sent away to another space, creates the paradoxical presence of an absence. Nico's bodiless territory of domination over Mamá, Laura, and Luis transcends any clearly defined temporal and spatial conventions. It invokes an atmosphere in which the spaces and times that are lived by each of the four characters are merging, where a present setting might become the echo of another character's past experience, or which might change into the image of another's projection into the future.

Manuel Antin's film conveys the *atopoi* of Luis's feeling of being caught in between the immutable Buenos Aires of his youth and the impenetrable Paris of his present life as well as the expanding and traumatizing territory of domination of the dead brother, all described in "Cartas de mamá" through various technical devices. Filmed scenes through mirrors, insertions of past "stills" in a present setting, such as photographs and Laura's portrait, and the alternation of darkness and light present a plurality of moving spaces on the screen. The sharp juxtapositions of certain scenes, flashbacks and flash-forwards, and the sonic device of the voices off-screen further intensify the atmosphere of an invisible presence in a space that is lacking its traditional spatial characteristics.

Cortázar's short story about the experience of the interstice has itself traveled to different places during the past fifty years: from the Paris of the late 1950s to Buenos Aires, where it was first published and adapted by Antin in the early 1960s, and from there to Spain, where Miguel Picazo made the film *Cartas de mamá* in 1978.[13] This was not Picazo's first foray into the field of cinematographic adaptation. Besides *El hombre de la esquina rosada*, the film on Borges's short story that I have discussed previously, Picazo also adapted Miguel de Unamuno's *La tía Tula* (Aunt Tula) [1964] and *El hombre que supo amar* (The Man Who Knew Love) [1976], based on a José Cruset novel.

In contrast to the radically black screen, followed by a setting in Buenos Aires in Antin's work, Picazo's filmic narration begins in the apartment in Paris, with Luis and Laura lying in their bed. This opening scene is accompanied by tango music.[14] Luis gets up and walks over to a window. While he is looking out, his facial expression is puzzled. In the next scene, now in the bathroom, he stares at his face in a mirror, again with a perplexed gaze. In the corridor, the concierge gives him a letter. Before putting it into the pocket of his coat, he looks at it for several seconds, with the same facial expression. The scene changes again and shows a spacious living room, filled with antique furniture. An old woman (Mamá) is looking out on the street through a window. Then, the camera shows the mother in the garden, silently reading a letter, followed by a scene with Luis, who is holding a (the same?) letter in his hand, while the mother's voice names the source of the trauma: "Esta mañana Nico preguntó por ustedes." Next, Luis is riding the bus with the envelope in his hand. The city landscape passes by, while he languorously stares at the reflection of his image in the window. Then, the face in the window alters, until Luis looks, not at the reflection of his own face, but at Nico's (see fig. 4.1).

Fig. 4.1. Still from *Cartas de mamá* (dir. Miguel Picazo, Films for the Humanities and Sciences, 1978). While Luis is reading Mamá's letter on the bus, the reflection of Nico's face appears in the window.

These first minutes of the film already set a tone that is clearly different from *La cifra impar.* While Antin's camera moves slowly over the faces of the characters and lingers on the surfaces and tiny details of the objects, all in black and white, Picazo's color film is of a more fluent rhythm. With fewer close-ups and no drastic alteration of light and darkness as in Antin's filmic version, it shows the characters from relatively unambiguous points of view. Picazo's *Cartas de mamá* relies more directly on Cortázar's text. For instance, it includes a scene with Nico's funeral, where the uncle harshly accuses Luis: "es una vergüenza… quitarle la novia a un pobre enfermo." On the contrary, none of the characters in the Argentinean's film expresses verbally the reason for Luis's and Laura's suffering. A common technical device of both films is the use of the off-screen voices. To a lesser degree than Antin, Picazo also includes juxtapositions of scenes in his filmic narration (flashbacks, flash-forwards, and alternating settings of possibly simultaneous actions). Like Antin, Picazo shows numerous sequences with alternating settings (Buenos Aires and Paris, as well as several shots in one city), although not as sharply juxtaposed as in *La cifra impar.*

The initial sequences of *Cartas de mamá* introduce a motif that will become increasingly significant as the film evolves. This is the view through a window in the anonymous city. This element conveys the idea of Luis's sensation of being in a disquieting place in-between fixed boundaries—neither in the Paris of his actual life nor in the Buenos Aires of his past. Many shots of Picazo's film show windows—some with the characters looking out of their houses or apartments (for instance in the initial scenes when Luis and his mother look out of the windows of their homes), others where they are staring into a window from the street (as in a scene when Laura is strolling around Paris and tries to catch sight of the interiors of the houses). In other scenes there is no character looking into or out of a residence, but the film camera itself does. What distinguishes an ordinary description or cinematographic shot from a description or a shot filmed through a window? Most generally, a window connects an interior with an exterior space. It exposes a part of a room that would otherwise remain veiled to the passers-by.

The gaze through windows, this special kind of scopophilia, emerges in specific surroundings; it is characteristic of the urban city dweller. As a literary motif, these window-looks are significant in narrations of lonely subjects in the anonymous, industrialized cities of the beginning of the twentieth century. Roberto Arlt's Erdosain from *Los siete locos* (*The Seven Madmen*) [1929], for instance discovers the "asquerosos interiores" (8) of Buenos Aires while he is walking through the streets and glancing into the illuminated windows from outside. These random glances into the interiors alter the entire urban space for the protagonist. Buenos Aires now becomes a "zona de angustia," where the sensation of anguish, like a harmful gas, is spreading out, "penetrando murallas y atravesando los edificios" (9). In the collection *Poeta en Nueva York* (*A Poet in New York*) [1929–30], Federico García Lorca's lyrical voice, wandering through the dark streets in the US-American megalopolis, describes that "Detrás de la ventana, / con látigos y luces, se sentía / la lucha de la arena con el agua" ("Ruina," *OC* 2: 439). This window, instead of showing details of a cozy domesticity, conveys the idea of a scene of torture and suffering. Louis Aragon's more cheerful peasant in *Le paysan de Paris,* strolls around in a different set of urban spaces with windows, the Parisian passages. For him, the roofed arcades are sites of accidental encounters and of sudden aesthetic pleasures: "Un marchand de cannes sépare le café du *Petit Grillon* de l'entrée de l'immeuble… Tout un art de panoplie dans l'espace est ici développé: les cannes inférieures forment des éventails, des supérieures s'entrecroisant en X penchent vers les regards, par l'effet d'un singulier tropisme, leur floraison de pommeaux…" (20–21). Aragon's awed narrator begins to dream about the other passengers' and the inanimate objects' lives. The glimpses are enriching and almost intoxicating to the narrating subject. Besides their heterogeneity, the gazes in Arlt's, García Lorca's, and Aragon's texts all belong to isolated subjects, immersed in a city that they cannot understand. According to the theorist Heinz Brüggemann, it is precisely the sensation of loneliness in an anonymous urban surrounding that leads to this special practice of looking, of lingering on the surfaces and peeking into or out of a window.

> The view through a window… is a form of perception of the lonely subject of the big cities. The stance… of the observer…, who examines the… windows, is an aspect of his melancholic experience: as a breaking off of all living and active communication with the outside world, as a retreat into the self… The paradox of this form of perception implies that it is in this space

> of self-reference and of reference to the other… where the productive imagination, both the compulsions and the spontaneity of imagination, unfolds. (10; my translation)

This loneliness of the characters with regard to other human beings and their disconnectedness from the anonymous megalopolis and from themselves is also a key narrative element in Cortázar's, Antin's, and Picazo's works. While Antin conveys the theme through scenes with two or more characters who do not communicate verbally, Picazo's characters are often shown by themselves, alone with their inner visions and traumata. In the relatively few scenes with several characters, corporeal interaction or even eye contact is rare. Luis is repeatedly filmed sitting in public spaces such as cafés, in the bus, or in the Metro, staring outside the window with a reclusive expression on his face, while he is reading Mamá's letters or writing back to her. *Cartas de mamá* presents the characters in complete isolation, caught in their individual worlds, glimpsing each other through windows without being capable of communicating. In one of the final sequences, Luis is sitting next to a glass window in a café inside the Saint Lazare train station. It is the day of Nico's supposed arrival in Paris. Like Antin, Picazo presents this sequence in detail, although he does not repeat the shot several times. Luis's gaze lingers on the people walking by until he catches sight of his wife. She does not notice him. In this sequence, Laura becomes the female equivalent of Edgar Allan Poe's "Man of the Crowd," who is fervently rushing through the masses, driven by an interior force. Respectively, Luis might be compared to the narrator of Poe's story, who sees without being seen (like the audience in a movie theater). Just as for Poe's narrator, Luis's fascination with the passerby does not lead to an understanding of the other. Poe's "it will be vain to follow, for I shall learn no more of him" (109), could also describe Luis's thoughts. When Picazo's character returns to the apartment in the evening and hears Laura's lie—"No me moví de casa en todo el día"—, he remains silent. While pronouncing the sentence, Laura looks out of the apartment window, with her eyes lost in space. Both have given up all attempts to understand and to communicate with each other. The window, instead of opening up the view, throws Luis, who is sitting in the bus, back on himself. The opening and the closing shots with first Luis and at the end Laura looking outside the window of the apartment introduce and end the visual meditation on the motif of gazes that search in vain and ultimately get lost in an *atopos* of unrest.

In the paragraph quoted above, Brüggemann further underlines in which ways the window-gaze conveys a nostalgic perspective. The nostalgic passerby aims at seeing a scene that he might have lived or imagined before, but is continually betrayed, since the scene never entirely coincides with his pre-established mental image. David L. Eng and David Kazanjian describe the phenomenon of melancholy, based on an analysis of Sigmund Freud's "Mourning and Melancholia" and Walter Benjamin's "Theses on the Philosophy of History": "Melancholia results from the inability to resolve the grief and ambivalence precipitated by the loss of the loved object, place, or ideal… [This] melancholy might be said to constitute, as Benjamin would describe it, an ongoing and open relationship with the past—bringing its ghosts and specters, its flaring and fleeting images, into the present" (3–4). In Cortázar's, Antin's, and Picazo's works, Luis arduously tries to convert the brother's invisible and traumatizing presence into a past memory, in order to overcome it. But his melancholic view prevails, in part as a result of his deep isolation.

In *L'espace littéraire*, Maurice Blanchot elaborates on the difference between a presence in melancholy and the memory of an irremediable past:

> Le souvenir est la liberté du passé. Mais ce qui est sans présent n'accepte pas non plus le présent d'un souvenir. Le souvenir dit de l'événement: cela a été une fois, et maintenant jamais plus. De ce qui est sans présent, de ce qui n'est même pas là comme ayant été, le caractère irrémédiable dit: cela n'a jamais eu lieu, jamais une première fois, et pourtant cela recommence, à nouveau, à nouveau, infiniment. … Le renversement qui, dans l'absence de temps, nous renvoie constamment à la présence de l'absence, mais à cette présence comme absence, à l'absence comme affirmation d'elle-même, affirmation où rien ne s'affirme, où rien ne cesse de s'affirmer, dans le harcèlement de l'indéfini. (21–22)

Blanchot presents memory as freedom from the past. On the contrary, the melancholic repetition of an action stands for a subject's lack of freedom. In all three versions of "Cartas de mamá," Luis's description of his predicament is in accord with Blanchot's discussion of memory and melancholy, for Luis compares his present situation with a "libertad condicional… libertad duramente conquistada" (*OC* 1: 251). Yet, the longed-for liberation far away from the house on Suipacha Street in Buenos Aires, ultimately fails. When the characters look out of the windows, they are unable to perceive an outlook into a future or a look back into a finite past. Their gazes only capture, to use Blanchot's words, "the presence of absence" of Nico's territory of domination. Picazo shows this invisible presence indirectly through the eyes of his protagonists who endeavor to perceive but fail. In the initial scene, Luis is scrutinizing the surroundings as well as his mirror image in order to discover the source of the sound that woke him up. He does not gain any insight. In one of the final sequences, Laura's and Luis's gazes are simply lost in space.

Picazo's characters increasingly distrust their sense of vision. This distrust is shown on the screen in sequences where a character suddenly sees another character at a certain place, and immediately afterwards sees the place again, deserted. In an early shot, for instance, Luis is sitting in a café with the troubling first letter from his mother. He does not want Laura to know about Mamá's *lapsus linguae*, and therefore re-reads it outside the apartment. All of a sudden, his wife is sitting next to him. Luis looks up from the paper, startled. A second later, the camera shows the identical scene from the same point of view, now without Laura. Luis also thinks that he glimpses his dead brother in Paris. While he is writing a letter to Mamá in a café, he stares out the window and discovers Nico, with a suitcase in his hand, looking at him, as if he were waiting for Luis to come out and welcome him. The following shot shows the scene on the busy sidewalk again, now without the brother. These shots are not only disconcerting for the characters, but also for the viewers, who have seen Laura and Nico for a few seconds, before the screen shows the deserted spaces again. Like the characters, viewers may doubt their visual perception and come to accept the possibility of an invisible force, or even of the presence of the ghostly brother, Nico.

Cortázar ends his short story with Luis's inner monologue on the presence of the dead. Nico was and remains "el amo en el territorio blanco y tibio de las sábanas" (*OC* 1: 269). Antin concludes his film with Luis's voice off-screen. The name of the brother, uttered through the bodiless voice, is expanding in space, and taking possession of it: "Nico está… siempre estuvo…Tan en todas partes..." Compared to the two former works, Picazo's film is again more explicit. At the end of his *Cartas de mamá*, Luis clearly utters his frustration. The spouses are in their bed. Without looking at his wife, Luis says: "No hay nada en vos ni en mí que no sea Nico." Laura, again, remains silent. In the final shot, now in the living room, the spouses are facing each other, from opposite sides of the room. With tears in her eyes, Laura asks: "¿No te parece más flaco?" (referring to Nico) whereupon Luis replies: "Puede ser. En dos años la gente cambia." The final take shows Laura and Luis standing on both sides of the empty sofa, at the very margins of the frame. The camera focuses on the empty space between them (see fig. 4.2). The sound track registers their forced silence. The impact of Nico's invisible presence in the center of the room is shown indirectly through the characters' reactions toward it and through their gazes that over and over again attempt to catch sight of the melancholic presence of Nico's absence.

The challenge to transform Cortázar's literary descriptions of a traumatic interstitial non-space formed of guilt and melancholy

Fig. 4.2. Final shot from Picazo's *Cartas de mamá*, with Laura and Luis in their living room, both looking at the invisible protagonist Nico at the center (dir. Miguel Picazo, Films for the Humanities and Sciences, 1978).

into a flow of images has had highly creative results. Both Antin and Picazo convey the disquieting atmosphere and Nico's invisible presence between the spouses. Since I consider the indirect invocation and the invisible and silenced presence of the brother as one of the main elements in Cortázar's text, for me, Antin's film is a more subtle and adequate response than Picazo's. Yet Picazo emphasizes the couple's loneliness via their gazes through windows, a key element for the nostalgic substrate of the text and the film. Thus, to varying degrees and with different technical devices, Cortázar, Antin, and Picazo all display the disquieting atmosphere of the traumatic presence of the absent brother.

In a letter to Antin, Cortázar commented upon the draft of a novel Antin had written and sent him.[15] Cortázar admired the ambiguity of the situations and highlighted the protagonists' disquiet as a reflection of the human feeling of defenselessness in amorphous surroundings.

> Sabés, lo que me impresionó en tu novela… es la ambigüedad casi insoportable de [la] situación. … Es esa ambigüedad esencial que los [a los personajes] vuelve vertiginosos y, sobre todo, nos denuncia. Vertiginosos porque son embudos, porque a través de sus conductas absolutamente imprevisibles, sospechamos el enorme flan de sémola sobre el que estamos parados y que a fuerza de conceptos, ideas recibidas y optimismo acabamos por creer un terreno sólido… ese territorio ambiguo y monstruoso… (Cortázar, *Cartas 1937–1963* 503)

Cortázar the critic draws attention to an aspect of a friend's literary text that I read as a main element of his own literary writings, among them "Cartas de mamá." The apparently solid ground in Laura's and Luis's life-world in Paris shows itself to be an unreliable and adverse space, similar to the metaphorical "flan de sémola" Cortázar sees in Antin's text. Both Antin's *La cifra impar* and Picazo's *Cartas de mamá*, each in its own way, conjure the atmosphere in an ambiguous territory and the dominance of an invisible force on the cinematographic screen.

Chapter Four

Echoes in the Dark

Pedro Páramo on the Page and on the Screen

In the novella *Pedro Páramo* (*idem*) [1955], Mexican author Juan Rulfo creates a desolate village on the prairie, haunted by whispers and apparitions. His Comala is doubtlessly one of the most disquieting and radical non-spaces portrayed in Spanish American literature. Rulfo's bibliography is brief. In 1953 he published the collection of short stories *El llano en llamas* (*The Burning Plain and Other Stories*), followed two years later by *Pedro Páramo*. His third and last work, the collection of three filmscripts *El gallo de oro y otros textos para cine* (*The Golden Cock and Other Filmscripts*), is from 1980.[1] The impact of his texts on the Mexican as well as the international reading public has been immense. *Pedro Páramo* was published and republished by all main Latin American presses, and was translated into more than twenty-five languages within the first twenty years after its publication. Most critical studies of the novella focus on the structure of the narration, the use of symbols, and the presentation of time. The subject of space as an element of the literary discourse, rather than merely as the symbol of an extratextual reality, has received less critical attention.[2]

The spaces and ambiances of Rulfo's texts are poor rural environments exposed to extreme climates such as heat, earthquakes, or torrential rainstorms and flooding (Martín 130; Valadés 8). *El gallo de oro* opens with a description of a dusty and deserted space: "Amanecía. Por las calles desiertas de San Miguel del Milagro, una que otra mujer enrebozada caminaba rumbo a la iglesia… Algunas más barrían las polvorientas calles" (21). The plains in the short stories in *El llano en llamas* are rocky and desolate. The characters are scuffling over the dusty soil and stumbling across arid furrows. The soil in "Nos han dado la tierra" ("They Gave Us the Land"), the initial text of the collection, is a "llanura rajada de grietas y de arroyos secos" (*OC* 37). The narrator, who has been walking in the heat for many hours, suddenly sees a drop falling on the ground. The description of this detail characterizes the entire ambiance of barrenness and infertility: "Cae una gota de agua, grande, gorda, haciendo un agujero en la tierra y dejando una plasta como la de un salivazo. Cae sola… No hay ninguna más. … Y a la gota caída por equivocación se la come la tierra y la desaparece en su sed" (*OC* 38). The personified soil is seared to such a degree that the drop of water only augments its thirst. The ground never serves as farmland. The only time when the characters are turning over the soil is when they are burying their dead. The narrator in "Talpa" describes how he and his lover buried the corpse of a man they had killed (*OC* 72). Far from being a holy ground for a deceased person's remains, the well is just a hiding place for a stinking cadaver. The narrator in the story "Anacleto Morones" (*idem*) describes in detail how he weighted down the grave of a man he had killed with heavy stones: "'¡Que descanses en paz, Anacleto Morones!' dije cuando lo enterré, y a cada vuelta que yo daba al río acarreando piedras para echárselas encima: 'No te saldrás de aquí aunque uses de todas tus tretas'" (*OC* 170). The dead man is a revenant who has to be weighted down and kept in the subterranean prison by the burden of heavy stones. In Rulfo's narrative universe, the underworld is the place of potential events.

In addition to these expressive spaces that are reminiscent of the sites of the high modernist literary tradition (such as Kafka's *The Trial*, where the protagonist K., accused of an unspoken crime, is killed in a dark quarry), Rulfo also creates *atopic* sites that lack clear spatial demarcations. Several texts of *El llano en llamas* describe extremely unstable terrains that become characters in themselves. The narrative voice in "El día del derrumbe" (The Day of the Landslide) remembers an earthquake: "Vi cuando se derrumbaban las casas como si estuvieran hechas de melcocha, nomás se retorcían así, haciendo muecas y se venían las paredes enteras contra el suelo. … La tierra se bandeaba todita como si por dentro la estuvieran rebullendo" (*OC* 142–43). Stirred like a sleeping animal, the ground bulges in pain, moved by an inner energy.

In *Pedro Páramo*, Rulfo intensifies the opaque and disquieting quality of space. As the title suggests (the name "Pedro" etymologically derives from *petra*, the Latin word for "stone," and the Spanish word *páramo* literally means "bleak plateau" in English), the story takes place in a stony, bleak, and deserted no-man's land.

At the beginning, a young man, Juan Preciado, is on his way from a city to his mother's home town, Comala. On her deathbed, she told him to go meet his father and demand his inheritance. While Juan approaches the valley, together with a muleteer as his guide, he describes his first impression of the place:

> nos íbamos hundiendo en el puro calor sin aire. Todo parecía estar como en espera de algo.
>
> — Hace calor aquí— dije.
>
> — Sí, y esto no es nada— me contestó el otro —... [Comala] está sobre las brasas de la tierra, en la mera boca del infierno. (67)

Comala is a vacuum, a site of extreme heat, hence outside of ordinary human reality. In an interview, Rulfo explained what made him choose the name. It is a "derivación de comal —comal es un recipiente de barro, que se pone sobre las brasas, donde se calientan las tortillas—, y el calor que hay en ese pueblo, es lo que me dio la idea del nombre. Comala: lugar sobre las brasas" (*Biografía armada* 61).[3]

The hell of Comala, however, bears little resemblance to previous literary spatial invocations, such as Dante's *dystopic* depiction of the inferno in *Divina Commedia.* As Jean Franco points out: "The topography of Dante's hell—the walled cities, the deep precipices, and the plains aflame—reflects the rigid destiny of the damned and the diversity of the sins to be punished" (430). Rulfo's hell, on the contrary, is not divided according to a strictly hierarchical and clearly perceivable order. It is chaotic, and therefore even more disquieting. It also lacks its traditional counterpart, paradise, the binary opposite that defines hell negatively. The heaven that appears in the novel does not reward for the tribulations of life. For example, the ghost of the old woman Dorotea recounts her stay in heaven in a dream, which she describes as a place filled with uniform angels, where a critical saint took a nutshell out of her stomach as proof that she never had nor would have a child. She was sent back to earth with the vague instruction: "Ve a descansar un poco más a la tierra, hija, y procura ser buena" (129). In this inverted worldview, earth is the resting place, and heaven a dull site of frustration. The Christian *topoi* of heaven, earth, and hell have undergone significant changes in Rulfo's narration.[4] The mouth of hell is a site of transition between an imprecise life and a hell that is equally vague. Juan Preciado describes it as a place where "todo parecía estar como en espera de algo" (67). This waiting is different from, for instance, the waiting for death in Beckett's *Waiting for Godot* written only three years before *Pedro Páramo*, where the figures are killing time to escape it temporarily. Death is no ultimate caesura in the novella; hence, the atmosphere of suspense and restless movement is even more absurd than in Beckett's play.

Michel de Certeau describes the *atopos* as "une manière de 'passer'" (155). For him, "marcher, c'est manquer de lieu" (155). In this respect, Rulfo presents a literary *atopos* of a new dimension—a site that is lacking spatial characteristics; a relentless passing as dying. Fabienne Bradu highlights the interstitial quality of a space in breathless tension: "[Comala es] el umbral que separa dos regiones, participando de ambas sin ser exactamente ninguna de ellas; un punto suspendido, un punto límite entre el adentro y el afuera de la tierra. En la *mera* boca del infierno, es decir un punto 'entre'" (*Ecos* 12; emphasis in original). The mouth facilitates the passageway both from life to hell and from hell to life, without belonging to either of the two realms. It is through this gate that human beings, and among them young Juan Preciado, descend to hell. The passage is also the site where the voices from hell pass to communicate with those who are still alive. The transcription of these voices at the gate to hell, both from inside and outside, forms the textual corpus of *Pedro Páramo.* What "takes place" in Comala is the intermingling of bodiless voices descending to the underworld from higher levels with others that are rising from deep down. Comala is a resonating chamber for the chorus of voices. It manifests itself as a site of imprecision (Bradu, *Ecos* 12), made of dreams, illusions, and haunting echoes.

The "lack" of a recognizable space, and the characters' feeling of being lost in space, have fundamental implications for the conception of the individual in the text. The characters, unable to find a stable spatial referent, lose their own corporeal boundaries. Juan Preciado, in his quest for his father, is guided to the town by his dead mother's voice. Her nostalgic remembrances invoke a paradisiacal Comala, embedded in a "llanura verde, algo amarilla por el maíz maduro. De allí se ve Comala, blanqueando la tierra, iluminándola durante la noche…, un pueblo que huele a miel derramada" (66, 80). For Jean Franco, "Comala as a paradise exists on the auditory level" (434). I would like to add that Juan Preciado, when wandering toward the place, is not only guided by his mother's voice, but also by his own mental images of a Comala of his longing. "Comencé a llenarme de sueños, a darle vuelo a las ilusiones. Y de este modo se me fue formando un mundo alrededor de la esperanza que era aquel señor llamado Pedro Páramo, el marido de mi madre. Por eso vine a Comala. … Me trajo la ilusión" (65, 119). But the hope to encounter his father in a mundane Eden flowing with honey will be betrayed. The more Juan approaches the village, the more his mental image corrodes. Comala kills all hopes, as well as the lives of its inhabitants and visitors. It is a foul-smelling, gloomy setting, filled with bad omens (66–67). The muleteer Abundio's commentary reinforces this atmosphere of bad presentiments. He turns out to be Juan's half-brother, and laconically summarizes that "nuestras madres nos malparieron en un petate" (68). However, Juan Preciado's senses are not yet adapted to the new surrounding. He has trouble hearing Abundio's voice, and cannot see clearly. When Abundio murmurs: "Váyase mucho al carajo" (69), Juan does not understand the curse, which can be taken as a prophecy. At this point, he does not even realize that he is talking to a dead man.

When the young traveler arrives at Comala, he is still unable to hear its sounds and noises. But at that moment he feels[5] that the space is rife with sounds, and that he is simply not sensitized enough to perceive them (71). Not only his senses of hearing and sight, but also his sense of touch has to adapt to the new environment. For instance, he attempts to open the door at the entrance of Eduviges's house, but this simple gesture fails, as the door magically flies open without being pushed (71). Juan Preciado's account is stamped by his uncertainty with regard to the adverse space. Consequently, as José Carlos González Boixo remarks, "siendo él el narrador, no puede ofrecer otra visión que la de la incertidumbre en que se encuentra en ese momento" (introduction to *Pedro Páramo* 39–40). Comala's inhabitants act differently from any human beings Juan Preciado has met before. For instance, he observes an old woman who appears and disappears suddenly, "como si no existiera" (70). She is a revenant, roaming through the deserted Comala. As a result of these unusual encounters, Juan Preciado finally accepts (without understanding) that he has to abandon all former experience.

In response to the novel environment, his body radically alters. "Me sentí en un mundo lejano y me dejé arrastrar. Mi cuerpo, que parecía aflojarse, se doblaba ante todo, había soltado sus amarras y cualquiera podía jugar con él como si fuera de trapo" (73). In the new space, the laws of gravity are abolished. Juan Preciado loses physical control. His body expands. Later, it will dissolve entirely. The novel describes several changes of human bodies such as Juan's. For instance, the body of the old beggar Dorotea becomes asexual and shrinks, so that she fits in the inside of Juan Preciado's elbow, while both are sharing a grave (120). Another woman who gives Juan shelter is described as melting into a puddle of mud (116). The final example of a human body that radically alters is Pedro Páramo. When he dies, his body, "se fue desmoronando como si fuera un montón de piedras" (178). Although the surrounding space of Comala does not actively destroy its inhabitants, the adverse ambience of a village in suspense, filled with torrid heat, clearly promotes the expanding, melting, shrinking, and falling into pieces of their bodies. These corporeal changes echo the Ovidian metamorphoses. As in the classical text, a superhuman power transforms a human being (often in the form of a punishment), which nevertheless retains his/her human consciousness and spatio-temporal continuity (Bynum 28; Segal 9–11). However, a striking contrast to the classical model in *Pedro Páramo* is the outcome of the metamorphosis. Instead of becoming trees or animals, the characters in Rulfo's text "spatialize." If, in the words of Caroline Walker Bynum, "metamorphosis… is about process/mutatio, story, a constant series of replacement-changes…, it is about one-ness left behind or approached" (30), the Rulfian metamorphosed beings leave their one-ness behind, in order to merge with their surroundings.

The spaces in Comala are not described directly. They are evoked *ex negativo* via their inhabitants' corporeal changes and their frustrated efforts to reach and possess those spaces. All three of Pedro Páramo's sons are wandering through areas that are veiled to them. Juan Preciado approaches Comala without being able to see it clearly. Miguel Páramo is searching for an inaccessible place. He wanted to go visit his girlfriend in a village called Contla, but recounts that, "no pude dar con ella. Se me perdió el pueblo. Había mucha neblina o humo o no sé qué; pero sí sé que Contla no existe" (84). Abundio, the third of the cacique's sons, is equally lost in space. After his wife dies, he gets drunk in the tavern in Comala. When he wants to go back to his shack, he wanders under the influence of alcohol: "Trató de ir derecho a su casa… pero torció el camino. … siguió avanzando, dando traspiés, agachando la cabeza y a veces caminando en cuatro patas. Sentía que la tierra se retorcía, le daba vueltas y luego se le soltaba; él corría para agarrarla, y cuando ya la tenía en sus manos se le volvió a ir" (175). All his desperate attempts to capture the ground fail. For him, "moving erases the previous sel[f], or makes [him a] memory ghost" (Franco 433). None of the three sons arrives at his destination.

The non-space in Rulfo's text is furthermore delineated indirectly by means of acoustic signs. Sound waves travel through space and time, until they reach a barrier denser than the air that sends them back to the area they have passed through before. A wall reflects a sound, and therefore delimits the space the sound waves have crossed. Comala is a site of haunting voices, filled with the resonance of footsteps, squeezing noises, barks, sighs, and screams. During his first night in Eduviges's house, Juan hears frightening noises he cannot explain. The old Damiana later explains that there must have been "algún eco que está aquí encerrado. En este cuarto ahorcaron a Toribio Aldrete hace mucho tiempo" (94). The whole village "está lleno de ecos. … Cuando caminas, sientes que te van pisando los pasos. Oyes crujidos. Risas. Unas risas ya muy viejas, como cansadas de reír. Y voces ya desgastadas por el uso" (101). The voices and sounds of the souls in pain are merely instantaneous, floating and scampering in the resounding edifice of Comala.

Echo is the main element that indirectly evokes space (Estrada 85). Besides multiple textual references to the motif, it is also literally re-created in *Pedro Páramo*. Juan Preciado, while wandering through Comala with his guide Damiana, is suddenly alone. "—¡Damiana! —grité—. ¡Damiana Cisneros! Me contestó el eco: '¡…ana… neros…! ¡…ana… neros!'" (103). Furthermore, the novel contains structural echoes that consist in repetitions of certain sentences at the beginnings and ends of several fragments. For example, the initial sentence: "Vine a Comala porque me dijeron que acá vivía mi padre, un tal Pedro Páramo" (65) is echoed in the final sentence of the first fragment: "Por eso vine a Comala" (65). All these devices evoke a sonic Comala, pervaded by sound waves in perpetual motion, just as by their invisible emitters, the souls in pain. Rulfo's narrative voices, like the mere faceless voices of a chorus in a Greek drama, are commenting on former events. However, they do not make meta-commentaries like the chorus of a tragedy, but are instead the bodiless actors of this drama that takes place in a nowhere-space.

One of the main literary palimpsests of the haunting voices in the closed area is the Greek myth of Echo. Like the Ovidian metamorphosis, *Pedro Páramo* emphasizes the relation between a bodiless voice and petrifaction. The chattering nymph Echo was condemned by the goddess Hera to repeat only the last syllables of words spoken in her presence. She subsequently falls in love with Narcissus. Unable to express her feelings, Echo is spurned by him and goes to hide her grief in a solitary cavern, where she dies of a broken heart. Her bones turn into stone. Rulfo's version presents a multiplication of "Echoes" with their voices resonating in an edifice, similar to the former nymph's cave. But while the Greek nymph finds rest in final silence set in stone, the voices in Rulfo's narration keep on talking and filling the village at the mouth of hell, even after the characters have died. The voices exist independently from a human body (although not from a resonating space). Unlike the Greek Echo's passive repetition of syllables, the voices in Rulfo's version are active. They even possess the power to attract and kill the only living being that has entered their confined space. In the grave with Dorotea, Juan realizes that "me mataron los murmullos. … Me llevó hasta allí el bullicio de la gente y creí que de verdad la había. … Y de las paredes parecían destilar los murmullos como si se filtraran de entre las grietas y las descarapeladuras" (118). In Rulfo's refashioning of the myth, the murmurs of the dead are the real agents of the drama in Comala. The initial title of the novel was in fact "Los murmullos," before it became *Pedro Páramo* (Estrada 95).

One character in the novel, however, shares the antique Echo's silent mourning: From her grave, the voice of Susana San Juan, Pedro Páramo's only love, recounts a traumatic childhood scene. Her father wanted to explore a mine in search of gold. Since Susana fit through the narrow opening of the cave, he sent her down, tied on a rope. But the only objects she found were a skull and bones. When she touched the skeleton, "el cadáver se deshizo en canillas; la quijada se desprendió como si fuera de azúcar. … Entonces ella no supo nada" (147–48). After this traumatic encounter with the *memento mori* in the cave, she suffers from amnesia. Her voice, further on, will be a longing enunciation of a single remembrance (or imagining) of a night of love at the sea. Similar to the mythical Echo, Susana is repeating over and over again an insane and sinful discourse in the eyes of the characters that surround her. Her descent to the excavation becomes a sonic *mise en abyme* of the novel. The cave can be read as the small equivalent of the unsettling site of no clear spatial boundaries that nevertheless functions as a prison for its living and dead inhabitants. The incurable effect of this event is paradigmatic for all characters in *Pedro Páramo*. Juan, Dolores, Dorotea, Eduviges, Miguel and Pedro Páramo, Padre Rentería, Donis and his nameless sister and incestuous lover, Damiana, Ana, and finally Abundio are all on the search for a treasure: the invented golden past, the recovery of innocence, fertility, virginity, the encounter of love, the ability to forgive, the resuscitation of the beloved. But during their journeys to a site of the dead, they only encounter dust, darkness, and a resonating space filled with haunting voices. As in a musical piece, the motif of a lonely being in a constricted space of resonances that will finally perish is repeated in other parts of the novel, and reappears in the textual coda, with the death of the despot.

If Rulfo's novel were adapted to the stage, its setting, props (or lack thereof), and illumination might be similar to the staging of a Beckett play, such as *Happy Days* [1961], *Play* [1962], or *Not I* [1972]. Comala, like the setting in *Not I*, "es el infierno. Y también el cementerio. … un mundo subterráneo de fosas y nichos, donde las almas viven una vida paralela, posible y complementaria" (Sabugo Abril 419). In *Pedro Páramo*, most actions take place after "el cielo se adueñó de la noche" (95). The beginnings of several paragraphs, similar to stage directions, describe the darkness and the whispering voices: "La noche. Mucho más allá de la medianoche. Y las voces" (104). These voices, analogous to the voices of the speakers in Beckett's play, have no vocal characteristics or signs of individuation.

The readers of Rulfo's text are not provided any concise spatial description. Juan is surrounded by vague "carretas vacías, remoliendo el silencio de las calles. Perdiéndose en el oscuro camino de la noche. Y las sombras. El eco de las sombras" (106). Unlike any common narrative or dramatic *mise en scène* involving an active character or actor and an inanimate background space, in Rulfo's novella, "el pueblo vivía" (70). The apparently immutable surroundings become active forces, without entirely revealing themselves to the observers. The characters, faced with such disquieting and indescribable surroundings, recoil. Some of them petrify, others fall down on the ground and disintegrate. At the end of the novel, the agonizing Pedro Páramo feels that his inner body is changing according to the transformations of the surrounding space:

> Estaba acostumbrado a ver morir cada día alguno de sus pedazos… Quiso levantar su mano…, pero sus piernas la retuvieron como si fuera de piedra. Quiso levantar la otra mano y fue cayendo despacio. … El calor caldeaba su cuerpo… Sintió que unas manos le tocaban los hombros y enderezó el cuerpo, como endureciéndolo… cayó. … Dio un golpe seco contra la tierra y se fue desmoronando como si fuera un montón de piedras. (177–78)

Pedro's death is a sonic event. What remains of him is the sound wave of a bang, spreading out in the spacious body of the village. The character blends with the surroundings, echoing the Christian discourse of all human bodies' destiny to return to dust. Comala assimilates and transforms the body of its formerly most vigorous inhabitant. The end of the novel radicalizes the petrifying "objectification" of the character, and the "subjectivization" of the surrounding space.[6] What seemed to be a narration by the inhabitants of the town turns out to be a narration of and about the town as the final protagonist. Rulfo himself highlights the central role of space:

> [*Pedro Páramo* es] una novela que se presentaba, con apariencia realista, como la historia de un cacique y, en realidad, es el relato de un pueblo: una aldea muerta, en donde todos están muertos, incluso el narrador, y sus calles y campos son recorridos únicamente por las ánimas y los ecos capaces de fluir sin límites en el tiempo y en el espacio. ("*Pedro Páramo*, treinta años después" 6)

Several critics have stated that such indistinct and indirectly active spaces could not be visualized. Federico Campbell brings forward the argument that Rulfo's text could be adapted to a radio play,[7] but not to the cinematographic screen: "El medio de la radio…

comparte con la novela la ventaja de no mostrar nunca el rostro de los personajes. … Tal vez por haber exhibido el rostro —por haberlo recortado, fijado, identificado— no trascendieron del todo las dos pretensiones cinematográficas [de Carlos Velo y José Bolaños]" (39–41). Campbell's opinion underscores the authority of the literary text, and measures any further adaptation on the notion of faithfulness with regard to the written source. Although the medial possibilities of an exclusively sonic adaptation that is able to convey an intermingling of different voices and to literally present silence are compelling, the cinematographic medium equally translates the challenging text, although based not upon the criteria of fidelity to the text but of creative transformations.

Two cineastes—Carlos Velo and José Bolaños—rose to the challenge. As in the cases of the movies discussed in the previous chapters, the filmic translations of the textual universe are highly inventive.[8] The first cinematographic version of *Pedro Páramo* [1966] is a joint venture of filmmaker Carlos Velo and the authors Carlos Fuentes and Manuel Barbachano Ponce. The initial credits define it as a "cinedrama…, basado en el cuento 'Pedro Páramo' de Juan Rulfo." The term *cinedrama* highlights the medial consciousness of its creators. The movie is described as a theatrical acting out, presented on the cinematographic screen. This *Pedro Páramo*, according to its paratextual description, is a hybrid work beyond ordinary generic fields that inquires into its own medial conditions. In the opening credits, the screen presents photographs of the actors with their names in one margin and the names of their characters in the other, accompanied by their voices off-screen. The focalization and movement of the camera are reminiscent of a nostalgic observer contemplating blurred faces in a photographic album. It marks Velo's *Pedro Páramo* as a journey to the past, a filmic equivalent of the mother's sonic remembrance at the beginning of the literary text. Another paratext included at the beginning of the film is an epigraph from Calderón de la Barca's *La vida es sueño*:

> Idos, sombras, que fingís
> hoy a mis sentidos muertos
> cuerpo y voz, siendo verdad
> que ni tenéis voz ni cuerpo;
> … desengañado ya
> sé bien que la vida es sueño. (pp. 163–64, lines 2322–27)

In Calderón's play, the protagonist Segismundo is tormented by doubtful shadows that pretend to possess physical bodies and voices. This quote foreshadows the disquieting ambiance of the film. During the following 105 minutes, the young traveler Juan Preciado will encounter shadows, voices, and highly unusual human beings that will challenge his worldview, built on rationality and logic. Calderón's quote can also be interpreted as a metafilmic device. The cinematographic narration that is about to begin is marked as an artificially fashioned and shaped space, a work of passing shadows.

It begins in a chronological fashion with a scene of agony in a dreamlike setting. Juan is sitting at his mother's deathbed. Dolores tells her son to go meet his father and demand his inheritance. Immediately after she pronounces Pedro Páramo's name, she dies. In the next sequence, young Juan is wandering through a desolate wasteland with scarce, windswept plants and a stony ground. He stops, and looks at a picture of his mother. While his gaze lingers on the photograph, he hears his mother's voice, praising Comala's fertility. The sequences follow closely the descriptions in Rulfo's text; the dialogues are mostly direct quotes of the dialogues in the novella. The film focuses on the elusiveness of the place, parallel to the elusiveness of the father. The muleteer Abundio answers Juan Preciado's "¿Dónde puedo ver a Pedro Páramo?" with a mysterious: "Por todas partes. Pedro Páramo es un rencor vivo." But the seemingly omnipresent father is invisible. When looking for him, Juan Preciado even loses sight of Abundio, who disappears in a cloud of fog. Alone on a gloomy plaza, surrounded by the ruins of the former town, he asks his mother where she has sent him (his voice is speaking off-camera). Her voice replies that he has now reached the place,"que yo amé, donde quisiera vivir para la eternidad." His eyes express his disorientation in the present site, so deeply marked by the ravages of time. A white sun illuminates the desolate scene and paints dark shadows on the floor.

As in the novella, Juan seeks shelter in Eduviges's house. The old woman guides him along a gloomy passageway, with other corridors branching off on both sides. Juan glances into these halls. They seem identical to the one he is walking along. The presentation of repeated architectonic forms will be one of Velo's main devices to convey spatial unease. The young traveler moves hesitantly. He does not know if he has already been at a certain site, or if a present position is simply similar to a place he has passed through before. This feeling of an uncanny space—which is disconcerting precisely because it is vaguely familiar—is shared by the audience.

The presentation of architectonic variations and repetitions of certain forms is a spatial equivalent of the acoustic motif of echo in Rulfo's novella. Just as the repeating voices deconstruct the concept of a reliable instance that is enunciating a unique speech in a determined space-time, the repeating forms deconstruct the notion of a single setting that can be clearly determined and verified by its occupants. Eduviges guides Juan to a room that she has supposedly prepared for him. But this purported personal space is entirely empty and dark. To his puzzled look, Eduviges simply replies: "el sueño es un buen colchón," and puts her oil-lamp on the bare floor. Since this lamp is the only source of light in the scene, the setting suddenly darkens. The two characters' shadows increase until they fill the background wall (see fig. 5.1). The camera zooms

Fig. 5.1. Still from *Pedro Páramo* (dir. Carlos Velo, Clasa Films Mundiales and Producciones Barbachano Ponce, 1966). While Eduviges and Juan Preciado are talking, their shadows grow until they fill the background wall.

out until it captures the characters and the much bigger shadows in their entirety. When Juan crouches down close to the lamp, his shadow spreads out over the wall. At this point in the film, a second narrative frame opens.[9] In a flashback, Juan gets to know his father, as a young Pedro Páramo is about to get married to Juan's mother. The dark room in Eduviges's house, illuminated by a single light source, restages the famous Platonic cave from *The Republic*, one of the earliest pre-cinematographic settings (Plato and Chappell 230–32). Plato's allegory about the doubtful duality of the real versus the fictitious image parallels Velo's projection about a young man who has traveled to a place because of his dead mother's nostalgia and his own fantasies about his father. Juan (and the observers), bound to his fixed position and forced to look at a wall, is caught in the tension between conflicting and unstable perceptions of what is reality and what is fiction. The framing device that introduces the figure of the father also underscores the metafilmic inquiry as to the status of the presentation. Juan Preciado in a dark room is about to witness a secondary, artificial staging of the *persona* of Pedro Páramo.

While the camera focuses on Juan, sitting in the semi-darkness, Eduviges's voice remembers: "Ay, Pedro Páramo… Pedro Páramo… era muy catrín con su traje inglés." Juan's yearning for his father in the empty space, along with the bodiless voice, conjures the visual image of Pedro Páramo in the character's mind and on the screen. The next scene shows the young Pedro Páramo in an English suit. The landowner has come to Comala to meet the supervisor, Fulgor. At the very beginning of their dialogue, he states that "la tierra no tiene divisiones para mí."[10] His main endeavor is to dominate all the land of the Media Luna estate. He pursues his goal by marrying Dolores Preciado for her money and land holdings, only to send her away soon afterwards, becoming the sole owner of their common goods. In order to accumulate more land, he arranges the murder of Toribio Aldrede, the owner of the land next to his own. In most scenes, space is shown to be hierarchically distributed according to Pedro Páramo's will. Even his final ruin is presented as the consequence of his decision. After his love, Susana, dies, he asserts: "Me cruzaré de brazos y Comala se morirá de hambre." This presentation of space as a reflection of man's willpower contrasts with all other practices of space that are shown in the film: Whereas Pedro Páramo actively builds and destroys his territory, all other characters either feel lost in inscrutable, slippery, and adverse sites or suffer from domination and spatial oppression.

Susana and Ana are trapped in spaces of repression, built mainly by Bartolomé San Juan, Pedro and Miguel Páramo. Susana is lying in her bed with the door locked, when her father breaks the lock and enters the room. At this point, his abuse is only verbal. But when she is trapped in a cavern, it becomes physical. Unlike in the novel, in which she is alone in the cave, Bartolomé descends after his daughter, where he embraces her and starts to kiss her passionately. Susana's sole happy moment in the film, the few seconds showing a love scene with her lover Florencio on the beach, is immediately followed by his death. Back in the house, her father points to a funeral cortège that is passing along the road: "¿Lo ves? El entierro de Florencio. Murió en la mina. Lo llevan a un pozo de la mina." The cave, the site of Susana's initial encounter with the abstract notion of death, now engulfs her most intimate love-dead. From now on, she obsessively relives and reiterates the scene at the sea. The spacious world of her visions acts as the dialectic counterspace to the confined site of imprisonment and decomposition.

Father Rentería's niece Ana is shown in situations similar to those in which Susana is placed. Ana's father has been assassinated by Miguel Páramo. While she is holding vigil over the body, the old Dorotea approaches her. She insinuates that the spirit of Ana's father is still alive, and that she could meet him for a last goodbye. She convinces the girl to go see her father in the graveyard at midnight. The man Ana meets, however, is not her father, but his very murderer, Miguel Páramo, who traps and rapes her among the tombstones. Similar to the cave in the scene between Susana and her father, the graveyard becomes Ana's site of the entwinement of symbols of death and sexuality, and the place that marks her for her whole life and afterlife.

The graveyard, a central place in Velo's *Pedro Páramo*, reappears near the end of the film. It is again the site of an erotic encounter that ultimately leads to death. Juan, who has been roaming through the ruins of Comala, sits down on a stone. The camera zooms out, and the viewers recognize that he is sitting on a tombstone. Dolores's voice asks: "¿Dónde estás, Juan?" whereupon his voice off-camera replies: "Aquí… Me mandaste a un pueblo solitario… buscando a alguien que no existe… sólo para morir por tí." The mother's voice replies: "Hijo mío, estoy a tu lado… ¡Abrázame!" He turns around to the gravestone next to the one he is sitting on, and embraces it. "Madre, sabes a polvo." At that point the camera goes out of focus. The stone in Juan's arms changes its shape. For several seconds, it resembles a female body. Then, Juan Preciado and the tombstone are falling to pieces, mineralizing into grains of sand. In a final embrace, the mother has guided her son from the living to the dead. Both have merged with the soil of Comala.

When Juan is dying, the audience is confronted with a blurred image. Through this technical device, Velo re-creates the character's liminal situation on the screen: Just like the dying anti-hero, the spectators are unable to see and make sense of the situation. The blurred screen points to the impossibility of conveying the ultimate residence of the dead or a character's transformation. Far from Dante's entranceway to an underworld of concentric circles, Velo's mouth of hell is an inscrutable and elusive space, where the characters and surrounding objects lose their shape and become indeterminate. The blurred screen can also be read as a reminder of the shadow's fictive reality on the flickering screen, referring again to the Platonic cave. This interpretation is emphasized by another deathbed sequence. Susana, while staring directly at the camera, as if addressing the audience, says: "Somos todos una pesadilla y todos moriremos antes del amanecer." She challenges the supposed dual concept of a reliable outside reality versus a fictitious illusionary world of shadows and presents the perils of a naïve belief in the "reality effect" (paraphrasing Barthes's notion) of a certain arrangement of traveling light rays that are passed through a celluloid strip and stopped on a dark wall.

The film ends with the cacique's death. Pedro Páramo is sitting in his armchair outside his estate. Abundio approaches him and asks for money to bury his wife. Pedro wants to know his name. While Abundio pronounces the words, "Soy hijo de Pedro Páramo," he attacks his father and stabs him and the old servant, Damiana, to death. After the drunken murderer has staggered away, Pedro, or his ghost, slowly gets up anew (see fig. 5.2). "Voy, ya voy, Susana" are his last words before he breaks down and falls on the dusty ground. The camera recedes and rises up until the dead man has become a tiny black spot on the monochrome landscape. The viewers are leaving both the interstice of Comala and the fictitious cave of the *cinematographos*. The camera zooms out and up.

Fig. 5.2. Final scene from Velo's *Pedro Páramo*. Pedro gets up again after being stabbed to death (dir. Carlos Velo, Clasa Films Mundiales and Producciones Barbachano Ponce, 1966).

Pedro Páramo has shrunk to the size of a pebble in the wasteland, scorched on the "comal."

In 1976, ten years after Velo's visualization of the *atopos* of disintegrating bodies and haunting voices, Mexican director José Bolaños presented a second transformation of Rulfo's novel to the screen. In the opening credits of his *Pedro Páramo—El hombre de la Media Luna* (Pedro Paramo—The Man of the Media Luna), he directly mentions the text: "Argumento basado en la novela *Pedro Páramo* de Juan Rulfo." Not only the plot, but also Rulfo's concise wording is present. Similarly to Velo's film, in Bolaños's version, most of the dialogues are direct borrowings from the novel. Possibly, the confrontation with Rulfo's textual universe of scarce spatial descriptions and volatile narrative instances made both directors rely on the few precise narrative elements of the dialogues. If a text does not precisely name the speaking instances, or describe when and where an enunciation takes place, the dialogues or monologues themselves are among the few unambiguous elements to be reproduced on film. For both directors, the soundtrack is a central technical device. It turns the written words into sounds and presents the motif of echo without a dimensional loss.

The initial setting of Bolaños's film is similar to Velo's: the screen shows a dusty prairie of gray boulders and bare hills, and a few cacti. Before the viewers see Abundio, they hear his voice off-screen. A second voice is introduced, repeating "Oiga… oiga usted…," before the audience sees Juan's silhouette, running toward the muleteer from far behind. The voices precede the physical bodies. They also often remain after the characters have left the screen, such as in the following scene when the two men are walking away from the camera, disappearing behind a hill, while their voices are still audible.

In Eduviges's house, after she has shown the traveler his room, she hears a sound and opens a shutter. Miguel Páramo is sitting on his horse, looking at her from the other side of the barren window (he ignores Juan). He has come to tell her that he could not find his girlfriend's village, and worries that he has gone mad. Eduviges explains: "loco no eres, Miguel Páramo, sino muerto." Many late twentieth-century critical thinkers, such as Michel Foucault, Gilles Deleuze, Félix Guattari, and Fredric Jameson, have highlighted the fundamental role of the distribution and use of space in the shaping of power relations. The scene of Eduviges's and Miguel's dialogue could serve as an exemplary illustration of the mechanics of punishment, based on hierarchical oppositions and the use of specific spatial signs, as elaborated by Foucault. According to the critic, "l'art de punir doit… reposer sur toute une technologie de la représentation. … Il s'agit de constituer des couples de représentation à valeurs opposées, d'instaurer des différences" (*Surveiller et punir* 106). Eduviges's space is fixed and limited, just as the space of the Panopticum is an "espace découpé, immobile, figé. Chacun est arrivé à sa place. Et s'il bouge, il va de sa vie, contagion ou punition" (198). Miguel's gaze, on the contrary, is a "regard… disciplinaire sur [un] corps docile" (190). However, the hierarchical relationship between Eduviges and Miguel differs in one key element from Foucault's model of power. Knowledge, Foucault tells us, in the tradition of the Enlightenment, is a form of power. The one who is in the position to articulate knowledge emphasizes certain elements, and therefore shapes the surrounding world for others. Yet, in the present scene, knowledge and spatial power are not intertwined. It is the woman inside the enclosed site who knows and explains to the authoritative man what has occurred to him. Which other discursive legitimation of power, besides knowledge, reigns in Comala? In a debate on *Surveiller et punir*, Jacques Léonard elaborates on an element that, for him, is missing in Foucault's genealogical study of power structures, which is central in the context of Rulfo's and Bolaños's imagined worlds.

> [Je suis] surpris que M. Foucault n'insiste pas plus nettement sur l'héritage religieux dans l'entreprise de dressage et de conditionnement. … N'est-ce pas le catholicisme post-tridentin qui exclut, condamne, réprime toute sorte de rebelles? … D'où vient la théorie de la culpabilité qui recense et dramatise les fautes morales? … Le dressage du corps, n'est-il pas d'abord une entreprise cléricale? (13)

The following scene in the film (and fragment in the text) introduces this other force—a very conservative and bizarre form of Catholicism that has the power to subjugate those who know and to reaffirm the brutal spatial dominance of the ignorant. The screen shows the interior of a church. Miguel Páramo's corpse is lying on the floor, with the motionless mourners around him. The only character who moves through the coded space is Father Rentería. He possesses the performative power to judge: "Hay esperanza para todos nosotros… Pero no para ti, Miguel Páramo." At the end of the requiem, Pedro Páramo approaches the kneeling priest. It is still within the church, and with all the mourners behind him, that he enumerates his son's outrage: "Sé que usted lo odiaba, Padre, y con razón. El asesinato de su hermano, que según rumores fue cometido por mi hijo; el caso de su sobrina Ana, violada por él." He then puts some gold coins on the prie-dieu, while he asks the priest to forgive Miguel. Father Rentería remains motionless until after Pedro has left the church. Then, he gets up, picks up the coins, and says: "Él puede comprar la salvación. Tú sabes si éste es el precio… En cuánto a mí, ¡condénalo Señor!" After a silence, he concludes in tears: "Está bien, Señor, tú ganas." The poor and insecure priest depends on the ruler's financial protection and power of persuasion. Through the confessional act of enunciating his son's deeds on holy ground, surrounded by the believers of Comala, the cacique, dominating the clerical discourse and highlighting its lack of righteousness, presses the priest to redeem Miguel's soul.

In contrast to the novel and to Velo's film, the setting of the church is present in many scenes in Bolaños's film. It is a site of negotiation and ultimate reaffirmation of power. The church is also an extremely gendered space, dominated by the male observers. Women are shown in uncomfortable and inferior positions. When Father Rentería returns to the church, there are about twenty women waiting to confess. They are all wearing black, with their heads covered by long veils. Shown against the bright walls and below the life-size sculptures of the Saints that are all dressed in colorful robes, they do not seem to possess physical bodies. The non-color black almost transforms them into mere shadows that are surrounding the symbol of clerical authority. As the priest passes by the long line, they all kneel down. As soon as he sits down on the bench at the confessional, several female voices begin with the confessions of their sins. The scraps of their monologues intermingle: "Me acuso, padre, que ayer dormí con Pedro Páramo… que tengo un hijo de Pedro Páramo… que le presté mi hija a Pedro Páramo…" The name of the ruler, and therefore his law, pervades the confessional. In a perverse reference to the biblical "In the beginning was the Word, and the Word was with God, and the Word was God" (*New Jerusalem Bible*, John 1.1), the cacique's name and power are omnipresent. The women's acts of naming their relation to the *Ueber*-father of Comala functions as a means of self-protection. Father Rentería, with his eyes closed in pain and helplessness, absolves them all. In Bolaños's cinematographic universe, the ruler Pedro Páramo has filled the place of the deity. The Lord's house has been transformed into yet another of the ruler's houses, where the believers now praise his authority and fertility.

But in contrast to Velo's film, Pedro Páramo is not exclusively presented as the brutal autocrat. He is also a deeply melancholic and desolate subject. Several fragments of Rulfo's book consist of Pedro's remembrances and mourning of his lost love, Susana. Bolaños's main technical device that alludes to this mental space of yearning is again sonic. Every time Pedro Páramo is absorbed in thought and dreams about Susana, a certain musical theme is played.[11] Through the repetition of this theme in different volumes and pitches (reminiscent of Alfred Hitchcock's practice for the purpose of creating suspense), the audience begins to associate a present moment with former situations when the music was played. The sounding and resounding of the musical motif propel a "different spatiality. Such a richer sense of geography highlights the spatiality of music, and the mutually generative relations of music and place" (Leyshon, Matless, and Revill 4). The string of sequences with this background music shapes a mental site of remembrance within the *atopic* site of Comala.

Besides the use of sound, Bolaños presents Pedro in special settings in order to convey his mental sojourns to the past. At the beginning of these scenes, he is lying on his bed, looking at the birds above him through a skylight and listening to their cooing. One sequence developed out of introspection is a childhood memory involving Susana, with a kite flying in the air, accompanied by the voices of two children: "Ay… el papalote, ¡Susana, ayúdame! … Ya voy Pedro." The act of remembering, the stringing together of different images, creates a setting for a yearning that is different from all the other timeframes that reign in Comala. The last of the repeated scenes with Pedro lying on the bed occurs toward the end of the film. Susana now lives at his house, physically as close as she never was before, but he has realized that she is inaccessible. Caught in a perpetual delirium, she does not remember their shared childhood and is unable to even recognize Pedro Páramo when he enters her bedroom. The film presents his final mourning for Susana through the repeated images of him lying on his bed, languorously looking out of the roof window. This time, the camera is not inside the room, but films the character from outside through the blurred glass. Due to this positioning of the camera, his features and facial expression are vague. The camera position foreshadows the dissolution of Pedro's body and his final fusion with the surrounding space. In Bolaños's version, he will die in his bed.

Besides the places of Pedro Páramo's longing, Bolaños shows another set of spaces of evasion. Those are sites of inner estrangement and suffering, associated with Susana. Unlike Rulfo and Velo, Bolaños neither presents her traumatic childhood scene in the cave nor her father's continuing sexual abuse. Right from the first time she appears on screen, she defines herself as a crazy person. On the patio of the Media Luna estate, following Pedro's doubtful invitation, her father tries to convince her not to give in to the *patrón*'s desire: "[Pedro] es según sé la pura maldad. Y tú quieres acostarte con él. ¿Estás loca?" Her reply simply is: "Claro que sí, Bartolomé, ¿no lo sabías?" Caught in her lonesome inner world, she is apathetic and incapable of any social interaction. When Pedro welcomes her in a spectacularly decorated ballroom, with dozens of servants and a banquet, she neither sees the luxury nor recognizes her host.

In Rulfo's polyphonic text, Susana's confusing flow of thoughts and emotions goes as follows:

> Estoy acostada en la misma cama donde murió mi madre hace ya muchos años. … Creo sentir la pena de su muerte. Pero esto es falso. Estoy aquí… pensando en aquel tiempo para olvidar mi soledad. Porque no estoy acostada sólo por un rato. Y ni en la cama de mi madre, sino dentro de un cajón negro como el que se usa para enterrar a los muertos. Porque estoy muerta. Siento el lugar en que estoy y pienso. … Y los gorriones reían… ¿Te acuerdas Justina? (144–46)

This paragraph, again similar to a Beckett piece, disconcerts due to its volatility, repetitions, and illogical enumerations. The readers are first invited to create a mental image of a female character lying on the bed where her mother died; then they are informed that she is in fact lying in a coffin, and attempting to momentarily escape her loneliness by remembering her mother's death. Next, the narrative instance mentions her narratee Justina, although she has just stated that she is alone. In his presentation of the internal suffering of this mentally ill character, Bolaños used only a few traditional filmic devices that convey her state, such as rapid camera movements that express an inner vertigo, rapid zooming in and out, or abrupt cuts suggestive of her inability to focus on and understand a given situation. The element that mainly conveys Susana's psychosis is the *mise en scène*. After the banquet scene, she is repeatedly shown alone in her bedroom. The place is vast; one of its walls is indiscernible in the distance. Susana is lying in her bed, enveloped in a white mass of sheets and bedspreads. The four-poster, wood-frame bed resembles a massive cage; the white sheets seem to be tie fastenings. Susana moves in her delirium, causing the sheets and her long hair to wrap more and more tightly around her body. Above the character, directly in her field of vision, the ceiling has a circular stucco ornament roughly the size of the bed. The structure of this adornment is similar to the arrangement in the bed: The white stucco curves and bulges seem to reflect the folds of the bed and of Susana's bright hair. These repeated forms are spatial equivalents of her hallucinations. She is constantly fantasizing about the scene of erotic love with Florencio at the sea: "Su cuerpo… desnudo… y mi cuerpo se sentía a gusto… el mar ahí… y las olas dando golpes duros contra mi cuerpo blando." The setting reshapes this site of a past or imagined encounter with carnal forms and the waves of the sea. But the former place of joy and freedom has turned into its opposite: now, Susana is caught in a site of restriction and of petrifaction. Space has acquired psychedelic characteristics.

Across from Susana's bed, there is a passageway of arches (see fig. 6.1). This architectonic shape reflects the sonic motif of the echo. Several times, Susana is shown waking up from a nightmare and calling the name of her father. The only reply is the echo of her own voice, traveling to and fro in the corridor. The repeating vaults, besides being a site of echo, are also a spatial figure of Susana's pain of no ending. For her, there is no light at the end of the tunnel of her life, no visible vanishing point to which she might direct her eyes. In a dialogue with her servant Justina, she communicates her belief system thus:

Fig. 6.1. *Pedro Páramo. El hombre de la Media Luna* (dir. José Bolaños, Conacine, 1976). Still with Susana, looking at the passageway of arches.

— ¿Crees en el infierno, Justina?
— Sí, Susana, y también en el cielo.
— Yo sólo creo en el infierno.

Susana's individual psychic hell will persist beyond death, just as the sequence of vaults in her room continues without any visible ending, beyond her and the viewers' visual fields. This aisle of no end is her path toward death. The last time the viewers see her alive, she is running to the passageway. This scene is suddenly interrupted by the image of her funeral. After her dead body has been carried out of the church, Pedro Páramo returns to her room, caresses the sheets and lies down on her bed. Now he is looking at the stucco ornament above. Susana had already abandoned him long before her physical death, and left him alone in a space of a petrified remainder of a yearned-for *jouissance*.

At this point the narrative frame of Pedro Páramo's space-time ends. The camera shows again Eduviges and Juan Preciado in the empty room in her house. While she is closing the shutter, she murmurs: "la ilusión me hizo abrir la ventana." The last five minutes of the film present how Juan Preciado's assumed reality turns into yet another visual illusion, now with regard to the viewers in the movie theater. The characters on the screen succumb to misperceptions. Damiana Cisneros, guiding the young traveler to his father's house, tells him about the voices she has been hearing: "Parece que [los ecos] estuvieran encerrados en los huecos de las paredes o debajo de las piedras... sientes que te van pisando los pasos... voces ya gastadas por el uso... me acerqué y vi esto—nada... y nadie." The extradiegetic viewers may get the same feeling: After Damiana's "vi esto—nada... y nadie," the screen becomes blurred. Then, while Juan Preciado fearfully asks if she is alive, her silhouette and body dissolve. Lost in a space of ruins, haunted by voices, he runs toward an amphitheater where he falls down on the ground, dead. The final sequence shows Abundio, who is rushing up the stairs to Susana's room where he encounters his father, lying on the bed. He pulls out his knife, ready to kill Pedro Páramo, stabs him, but then he realizes that the man is dead. Abundio opens his father's shirt and grabs at his chest. When he pulls out his hand, it is filled with sand. The last shot of the film shows his hand in a close-up, with sand trickling through his fingers (see fig. 6.2).

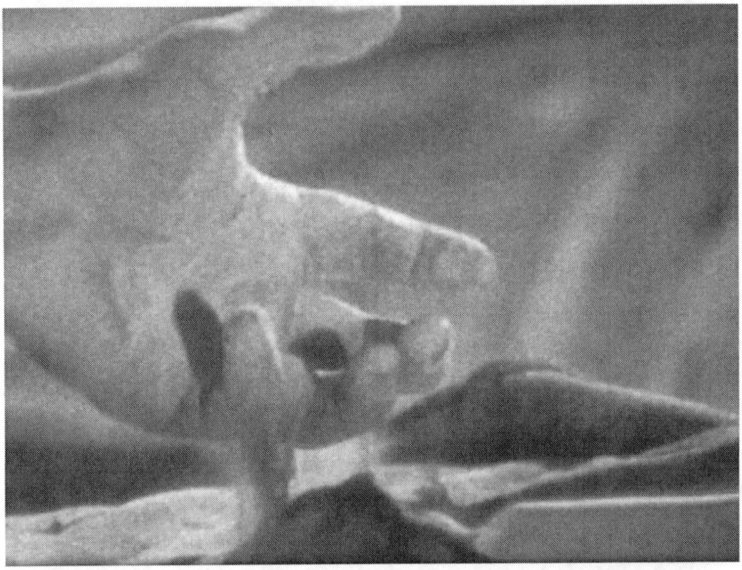

Fig. 6.2. Final shot from Bolaños's *Pedro Páramo. El hombre de la Media Luna.* Close-up on Abundio's hand, after grabbing at his dead father's chest, with sand trickling through his fingers (dir. José Bolaños, Conacine, 1976).

The death of the father is the climax in all three versions of *Pedro Páramo.* However, each film emphasizes different features of Rulfo's "se fue desmoronando como si fuera un montón de piedras" (178). Velo shows Pedro's body lying on the ground, literally collapsed after Abundio's knife thrusts. While the camera zooms out, he diminishes to a little, dark spot in the dusty surroundings. As the camera recedes and shows a panoramic view from above, he has become a mere dark spot on the landscape, similar to a pebble thrown on a bright surface. In Bolaños's film, Pedro dies mourning Susana's death, and therefore frustrates Abundio's longing for vengeance. The son can only touch the grains of sand and stare at the residuum of the passing of time. The final sequence of the film shows a "carpe mortem" where the sand, like in an hour-glass (the Spanish word for this is *reloj de arena*, or "sand clock"), runs through Abundio's hand.

In the novella, Rulfo's revenants of haunting voices appear and disappear in time and space, until they are silenced at (and by) the end of the text. The last utterance, the final narrative element prior to the white surface of the page, is the word *piedras* (echoing the first one from the title, the name "Pedro"). These stones could be rocks, dispersed across the wasteland; they could also be gravestones, mineralized remainders of human bodies that have disintegrated a long time ago. At the end of Juan Preciado's journey toward a world made of hope, there is nothing left but a dusty and stony ground. Space has annihilated its inhabitants. Velo conveys this radical situation through blurred screen images and extreme zoom-outs. Bolaños presents a body that only exists on the outside, but has long since corroded and mineralized.

All three versions of *Pedro Páramo* portray spaces that have lost their traditional characteristics of fixed and recognizable entities. They zoom in on the dissolving of boundaries, both spatial and corporeal. The interstice at the mouth of hell is evoked indirectly through its inhabitants' corporeal changes and via the resonating of the bodiless echoes that circumscribe their limitations. Space penetrates or fuses with the characters.

The features of a subject in motion (de Certeau's *passer*) in a space of no firm borders, where the notions of inside and outside have dissolved, are also characteristic of settings that seem at first sight incompatible with the fictional Comala. Postmodern cultural and urban studies highlight analogous experiences of space to those of Juan Preciado, Miguel and Pedro Páramo, and Susana San Juan. Among others, Fredric Jameson's analysis of the Bonaventura Hotel, Jean Baudrillard's description of Las Vegas, and Marc Augé's anthropological study of international airports use similar terms to describe the perception of a drifting, mirroring space and its occupants' feeling of getting lost in it. In Kathleen M. Kirby's words, "the shift from modernism to postmodernism entailed a shift in the disposition of boundaries. Modernism foregrounded boundaries to the effect of fortifying the interiority of the alienated self; postmodernism grants them such vividly phantasmagoric power that they have displaced… the dimensionality of whatever volume they once contained" (59–60). Rulfo's, Velo's, and Bolaños's Comalas are no postmodern sites and cannot be classified within the Western dichotomy of the modern and the postmodern; however, the spatial disquiet and fear of existential solitude on which the diverse, fictional, and critical accounts are grounded, are alike. And if Jameson admits to be "at loss when it comes to conveying the thing itself [the lobby of the Bonaventura Hotel], the experience of space you undergo" and is tempted to "say that such space makes it impossible for us to use the language of volume any longer" (*Postmodernism, or, the Cultural Logic of Late Capitalism* 42–43), he almost echoes Juan Preciado's initial impression of Comala. However, Rulfo and the two directors prove that the non-space can be told and shown and serve as an interpretive category and aperture through which a new fictional discourse can affect reality.

Chapter Five

Toward *Amor Vacui*

Gabriel García Márquez's and Ruy Guerra's *Eréndiras*

Gabriel García Márquez's "La increíble y triste historia de la cándida Eréndira y de su abuela desalmada" ("The Incredible and Sad Tale of Innocent Eréndira and Her Heartless Grandmother), from the 1972 collection of the same name, displays *atopoi* of openness in motion. Compared to the spaces in Borges, Cortázar, and Rulfo discussed in previous chapters, as well as to those evoked in García Márquez's earlier fiction, the sites in "Eréndira" are among the most challenging, both for the characters to interact with and for the readers to imagine.[1] The sites are perhaps the most radical physical manifestations of the human being's loneliness, a main theme in most of García Márquez's texts. Besides being a metaphor for human loneliness, space is a powerful and influential character in itself. Through the personification of this extreme non-space, García Márquez underscores the power of the surroundings over its inhabitants, as both an existential threat and an existentialist challenge.

Based on a real incident the author had heard of or witnessed,[2] the short story "Eréndira" develops a scene García Márquez had already included in *Cien años de soledad*.[3] He had also worked on a filmscript, without publishing it, before he chose the genre of short fiction to convey the "incredible and sad tale" of the innocent girl, forced into prostitution by the "heartless grandmother" to which its title alludes. After the initial misfortune when the wind of disgrace blows down a candlestick and sets the mansion on fire, the young protagonist and her grandmother become nomads. They wander a desert of no demarcation with no clear aim. Right from the beginning, this non-space is related to the characters' solitude. The grandmother's house is already situated in "la soledad del desierto" (97), "la impunidad del desierto" (99), "lejos de todo, en el alma del desierto" (98). This desert is portrayed as an amoral space beyond the realms of civil laws and morality. It is described negatively through its distance from everything, yet the narrator does not specify what this "todo" might refer to. The two characters do not communicate with each other. The grandmother does not talk, except for giving orders to her granddaughter, and is lost in a melancholic reverie of her past grandeur. Eréndira either affirms the commands with a repeated "sí, abuela" or remains silent. The narrative voice portrays the two characters as follows: "Mientras la abuela navegaba por las ciénagas del pasado, Eréndira se ocupó de barrer la casa, que era oscura y abigarrada, con muebles frenéticos y estatuas de césares inventados, y arañas de lágrimas y ángeles de alabastro, y un piano con barniz de oro, y numerosos relojes de formas y medidas imprevisibles" (98). In the abstract "space" of this sentence, the enunciation of the protagonist is "squeezed in" between the grandmother's account and the extensive enumerations and descriptions of all the objects in the house. Just as the syntax of the phrase indicates, Eréndira's task consists of helping to perpetuate the grandmother's nostalgic state in the museum-like assembly of remnants of her past splendor. Thus, the protagonist's space is initially constrained by, on the one hand, her grandmother's physical body and the authority of her voice, and, on the other hand, by an accumulation of objects that she cannot control or understand. Eréndira's entrapment and insecurity in this disquieting *atopos* will intensify as the narration develops.

After the wind of the protagonist's disgrace has stopped and the "refugio incomprensible" (99) of the house has been burned down, the grandmother makes Eréndira pay for the material loss she has caused. And as the girl's name indicates (Eréndira is phonetically close to "rendirá," the future form of the verb "rendir"), she will "render," "yield," and "surrender" to the power of the oppressive other. Several critics describe the relationship between Eréndira and her grandmother as one of slave/master (Penuel, Jain, Marting, Santos-Phillips).[4] This interpretation of the power connection of the young sex slave with the greedy procuress, representing the colonies and the gluttonous Spanish empire, is entirely convincing. In addition to this relation, I see a nexus of Eréndira with another "character." On many occasions, the short story describes the personified wind of disgrace as Eréndira's counterpart. Until the end, the natural element's practice of space is directly opposite to hers. Whereas the wind freely and actively travels through vast spaces and enters any closed sites, Eréndira is passively moved forward and perpetually entrapped.

The young girl starts to pay off her mishap when her grandmother takes her to the village store keeper. While the old woman is waiting for her in the store, Eréndira is raped in the back room. Her only resistance consists of a silent cry ("grit[ó] en silencio" 105). Right from the beginning of her abuse, she cannot speak to her oppressors. "With what voice-consciousness can the subaltern speak?" asks Gayatri Spivak provocatively, pointing toward the impossibility of the colonized subject's individual enunciation. Spivak concludes her seminal study on the limits of agency with the sketch of the task of the researchers: "The archival, historiographic, disciplinary-critical and, inevitably, interventionist work involved… is… a task of measuring silence" ("Can the Subaltern Speak?" 80, 82). Eréndira's sole resort is to escape into a somnambulant state, far away from the man next to her. Her readers are invited to "sound through" and interpret her silence.

The violence not only affects the protagonist physically; it also throws her into a different space. The man's "bofetada… la levantó del suelo y la hizo flotar un instante en el aire con el largo cabello de medusa, ondulando en el vacío" (105). Her clothes, violently stripped off, become "largas tiras de colores que ondulaban como serpentinas y se iban con el viento" (105). Her body reacts as if it were floating in the sea or lifted up in the air. Free from the force of gravity, her hair and clothes are flying in the invisible wind. In an offhand manner, the natural force partly liberates her from her state of subjugation. This is the first description of Eréndira floating in a space-time different from the spatio-temporal settings of the other characters. Besides underlining the radical exteriority of the experience of her rape, this passage points toward an invisible space of a potential emancipation.

The wandering of the young prostitute and her procuress starts when no more men in the village can pay for Eréndira's services. However, migration does not provide them with a new horizon. The horizon—I use the term both in the sense of a spatial limit between earth and sky and as a metaphor of human knowledge—gets increasingly blurred, as the grandmother and her granddaughter go off into the desert in search of new places. For instance, in the village San Miguel del Desierto, they only perceive the "polvareda del horizonte" (113). It is at this site of an indistinct horizon where Eréndira meets her later lover, Ulises. He is waiting for her in an inscrutable "espacio vacío y oscuro" (116), when the grandmother announces to all men waiting that Eréndira needs to rest and that they should come back the next morning. Late in the night, Ulises sneaks into the tent and approaches her:

> —Estaba loco por verte— …
> —Pero me voy a morir— dijo Eréndira.
> —Mi mamá dice que los que se mueren en el desierto no van al cielo sino al mar— dijo Ulises…
> —No conozco el mar.
> —Es como el desierto, pero con agua— dijo Ulises. (117)

Although there have been several allusions to the sea, the dialogue between Eréndira and Ulises is the first passage that directly names the sea as the desert's "other." Both are presented as boundless non-spaces, connected with death. The sea and the desert do not reveal themselves to the travelers who are surrounded by flat land, dunes, or repeated shapes of waves with no clearly distinguishable horizon. The iteration of analogous spatial forms and horizons causes the human beings' total subjection to space and prevents them from perceiving and understanding their surroundings.

Eréndira's wandering tent in the desert is similar to a ship in the vastness of the ocean. García Márquez uses the same image as Michel Foucault to elaborate on a spatiality that is fundamentally different from the *topos* or *u-* or *dystopos.* In his conference "Des espaces autres," Foucault defines the ship as the paradigmatic *heterotopic* site of spatial juxtapositions: "Le bateau, c'est un morceau flottant d'espace, un lieu sans lieu, qui vit par lui-même, qui est fermé sur soi, et qui est livré en même temps à l'infini de la mer" (762). Just as Eréndira is moved forward by her grandmother's greed and the fatal wind of disgrace, the mythical sailor Ulises is at the mercy of exterior forces such as winds, waves, and Neptune's lenience in order to reach the coast, return home, and thereby regain a stable horizon. The girl's young lover of the same name as Homer's sailor announces that whoever dies in the desert will have to endlessly travel the sea, this other space of no end and fixed horizon. By the end of the text, his premonitory words will have come true. García Márquez's heroine will not reach a home like Ithaca, but instead will incarnate the uncanny or "unhomely" non-space of the sea/desert and disappear into the distance, beyond any common spatial markers.

But prior to this, she will have to endure more sites of confinement and suppression. The fourth and fifth chapters introduce two sets of power structures and authoritarian places that have had a major role in Latin American colonial history: the missionaries, with the convent as the spatial symbol associated with them, and the settlers/colonizers, with the plantation as their space of exploitation of the human labor and soil. The missionaries capture Eréndira at night, wrap her in a mosquito net, "como un pescado grande y frágil capturado en una red lunar" (122), and lock her up behind the thick walls of the mission. As in former situations of physical abuse and spatial constraint, she reacts with inner distance and denies any form of communication. The subaltern in García Márquez's fictive universe does not even attempt to speak, to find her voice and recognize her own subjugation. Her lover, Ulises, suffers from a similar imprisonment in a space of authority and hierarchic distribution, which is his parents' grove of magical oranges that each contain a diamond. All attempts to steal a single orange from the immense plantation fail. Both of his parents watch him closely to discover the reason for his restless behavior. Like Eréndira, he refuses to speak.

After Eréndira is rescued from the convent, and after her frustrated attempt to flee from sexual slavery together with Ulises, the grandmother chains the girl to her bed of prostitution. This moment of Eréndira's most brutal exploitation is also the moment of her most splendid fame. Her tent of wandering love has a mesmerizing power over the men of the desert:

> [Delante de] la carpa del amor errante… la fila interminable y ondulante; compuesta por hombres de razas y condiciones diversas, parecía una serpiente de vértebras humanas que dormitaba a través de solares y plazas, por entre bazares abigarrados y mercados ruidosos, y se salía de las calles de aquella cuidad fragorosa de traficantes de paso. (145)

This image, which, according to García Márquez, has been at the origin of the short story, is highly puzzling.[5] First, the site of a brothel in motion undermines the traditional spaces of women in Latin American societies, which, according to Jean Franco, are all fixed and clearly marked: "Public space in Latin America was strictly separated from the private space of the house (brothel), home, and convent, that is spaces which were clearly marked as 'feminine.' These spaces gave women a certain territorial but restricted power base and at the same time offered the 'felicitous' spaces for the repose of the warrior" (12). Eréndira's residence, on the contrary, is an improvised house made of tarpaulin. Her restless traveling and short-term stays either make her clients hurry to meet her, or force them to passively wait for her. Her radical practice of space, running counter to the rigid compartmentalization of the supposed feminine spaces, prompts a new practice of space by the men. While they are waiting to enter Eréndira's tent, all their bodies merge into a "serpiente de vértebras humanas que dormitaba… por entre bazares abigarrados y mercados ruidosos, y se salía de las calles de aquella cuidad fragorosa de traficantes de paso" (145). This ekphrastic description of Eréndira's customers presents their practice of space as a shared and creative activity. All are participating in a new, meandering "body" that pervades and redefines the town. The serpentine line draws attention to the principle of improvisation and availability of space and indirectly of Eréndira's body. Ironically, however, the men's common, creative shaping of their surroundings is based on exploitation.

The other prostitutes in the village, who have been waiting for their clients in the clearly demarcated red-light district for several days, finally gather to go over to their rival, enter the tent, pick up Eréndira's bed, and carry it out on the streets. The other women reinstall authority and centrality: "La mostraron en su altar de marquesina por las calles de más estrépito, como el paso alegórico de la penitente encadenada, y al final la pusieron en cámara ardiente en el centro de la plaza mayor… bajo el sol terrible" (147). In the eyes of the other prostitutes, Eréndira has surpassed the limits between the public and the closed places; as a consequence, she is punished with an even more radical public exposure.[6] This is the only time that Eréndira is captured in an open space. Exposed to the collective gaze (including the narrator's), her body is branded by the stares of the surrounding villagers and, literally, by the atmosphere of torrid heat under a merciless sun. She is stigmatized in the political center of the village, the traditional male space, a recognizable and definable *topos*, in contrast to the *atopic* sites she was traveling through before, and where she will hide after this incident.

None of the many men attempt to rescue Eréndira. Would it not be in their personal and common interest to inhibit the public exhibition of the object of their desires, to shorten their waiting time and to send back the prostitutes to their assigned site? After Eréndira has been abducted, the crowd does not merely remain passive. Instead, it turns against her and mocks her. The men who have been waiting for the prostitute as the object, "placeholder" (Kaminsky 119), or "idea" (de Beauvoir 186) of their desire are suddenly confronted with the exploited subject.[7] In sharp contrast to the improvising shaping of spatial and corporeal forms, the naked woman, exposed in the common space of the central plaza, has ceased to be an object *for* the other; she has become a definite subject *among* other subjects in the public sphere. Therefore, the customers abandon their creative use of space and gather into an authoritarian crowd. In order to save face, they transform Eréndira into yet another, now collective object of adverse desire: She becomes the scapegoat of the whole corrupt town's remorse for taking part in her prostitution.

After this radical event, the grandmother and her granddaughter abandon the village and continue their nomadic life. Again, the girl endures a long chain of sexual abuses in total silence: "Eréndira se sometió en silencio al tormento de la cama en los charcos de salitre, en el sopor de los pueblos lacustres, en el cráter lunar de las minas de talco" (149), until she reaches the seashore. In her desolation, she silently calls Ulises, who hears her cries in his dreams back at his parents' plantation, and sets out once more to rescue her from the jaws of her grandmother. After several pathetic attempts, he manages to kill the procuress. This could be the end of an archetypal fairy tale or a mythical saga, if only Ulises would be more heroic and Eréndira would stay with him.[8] However, in García Márquez's ironic reworking of the genres, Ulises contradicts the figure of the mythological Odysseus or of the prince in a fairy tale in almost every way. As Christopher Little laconically puts it: "he is small, golden, lovesick, and ineffectual most of the time" (211). After killing the beast, exhausted by the fight and covered with green blood, this antiheroic hero even starts crying when he sees that Eréndira is running away from him. The text ends as follows:

> [Ella] corrió... contra el viento, más veloz que un venado, y ninguna voz de este mundo la podía detener. Pasó corriendo...

> por el vapor ardiente de los charcos de salitre, por los cráteres de talco, por el sopor de los palafitos, hasta que se acabaron las ciencias naturales del mar y empezó el desierto, pero todavía siguió corriendo… y jamás se volvió a tener la menor noticia de ella ni se encontró el vestigio más ínfimo de su desgracia. (162–63)

This ambiguous ending has been interpreted in diverse ways. For some critics, Eréndira's act is deeply ungrateful. Gene Bell-Villada notes that "she abandons her loving redeemer, for the sordid injustices she has endured have made her selfishly individualistic and opportunistic" (*García Márquez: The Man and His Work* 178). George R. McMurray even suggests that at the end she has become her dead grandmother's reincarnation (112). José Luis Méndez, in his dialectic analysis of the master/slave relationship, interprets her final act as the synthesis, where the protagonist assumes "valores y actitudes de su abuela, su sed de poder y sus ambiciones desmedidas. Por eso huye del amor y se pierde en el horizonte" (150). Christopher Little, on the contrary, reads the ending as Eréndira's positive self-affirmation, since she "runs back into the desert… to carve out her new life within the reality which she knows" (209). These contradictory analyses demonstrate one major element of the ending, which parallels the final portrayal of space—its radical openness.

The last paragraph describes the protagonist's escape toward an open horizon. She runs off the text and the fictional universe without leaving a single trace in space or a clear sign for the readers to interpret her movement. Such a spatial and interpretive openness can be disquieting. Yet it can also be an invitation to con- or post-fabulate beyond the limits of the short story itself. From the point of view of Eréndira's practices of space, her final elopement clearly differs from all earlier ones: For the first time, she is by herself, without any authority watching her. Also for the first time, she actively travels through space. She has even overcome the limits of gravity, is able to run over the surface of the water, and keeps on running further and further without any sign of exhaustion. Has she died and entered into a new space-time? According to Ulises's mother, the sea is the final space of those who pass away in the desert. The protagonist, however, does not aim toward the sea, but returns to and confronts her former space of oppression. By doing this, she affirms vitality. Through her different practice of space, she overcomes and literally surpasses these sites of pain.

Eréndira's use of space is clearly distinguished from that of the authoritarian characters, such as the missionaries who had built their monastery in the middle of the desert, or the grandmother who had created a microcosm of her own reign (the tent) within the endlessness around her, or Eréndira's suitors, who had mentally built a center of their individual universes (again, the tent) within the adverse desert of no ending. Unlike any other character, the protagonist does not attempt to install personal markers in the open space around her. Her movement affirms the space of potentiality. Her spatial praxis has now become similar to the praxis of her initially stated antagonist: the wind of her misfortune. As she challenges the wind ("corrió contra el viento"), she acquires its characteristics and becomes powerful, invisible, and ubiquitous.

The end of the short story describes the protagonist moving swiftly through an open space of shifting horizons. Dispersion and boundlessness have ceased to be negative terms. Eréndira ventures into a radical space where the former traces of her misfortune that are associated with spatial suppression vanish. Her final reaction is again not verbal but corporeal. She does not yell or shout, but instead silently and steadily passes through space (the gerund forms stress her perpetual movement: "pasó corriendo por…, siguió corriendo por…"). García Márquez's story of oppression ends with the subaltern's challenging of the structure of subjugation. It is no mere allegory of the fight between the strong and the weak, with the final victory of the weak, but instead a radical questioning of the dualistic concept itself. Eréndira is moving in a changing site of a dimension beyond common notions of speed ("más veloz que un venado"), authority ("ninguna voz de este mundo la podía detener"), space ("pasó corriendo por… hasta que se acabaron las ciencias naturales del mar y empezó el desierto, pero todavía siguió corriendo…"), time ("jamás se volvió a tener la menor noticia…"), and human perception ("ni se encontró el vestigio más ínfimo de su desgracia").

The repeated use of comparisons and superlatives shows the narrative voice's difficulties to seize and describe the sites beyond everyday perception. Similarly, the narrator's explicit statement of the incommunicability of the *atopic* desert of no horizon evokes the settings only negatively. The denial of any common experience (*topic* or *u-/dystopic*) indirectly points toward a space and perspective beyond the well-known boundaries of the page and the mind. The fictional *atopos,* either as a site of over-abundance, or as a space of void and invisibility, challenges the traditional belief in human understanding of the "fabric of physical spaces" (Kirby 15) and of an ensuing self-positioning in and in relation to them. The blank spot at the end of the text induces the readers to mentally create their own sites of radical exteriority and boundlessness. It also invites those readers, viewers, or listeners interested in intermedial relations to compare it with further creations of strange non-spaces of shifting horizons and radical boundlessness.

How is it possible to describe, show, and mentally understand a site of no limits through the necessary limited presentation in the literary and cinematographic media? One cinematographer who had to answer these questions was the Mozambique-Brazilian director Ruy Guerra. He presented his version of *Eréndira* in 1983. The film was the result of a joint venture of Guerra, the editor/cutter Kenouth Feltier, and García Márquez himself, who wrote the script for the Mexican-French-German co-production. Both the scriptwriter, García Márquez, and the director, Guerra, knew the respective other's artistic medium very well: García Márquez had initially aimed at being a cinematographer, and only after the process of writing *Cien años de soledad* did he dedicate all his creative energy to the literary medium.[9] Guerra, on the other hand, had started as an author of short stories and novellas before he chose film as his main medium of artistic expression.[10] As in the case of the films discussed in previous chapters, Guerra's *Eréndira* is no adaptation in the traditional sense. Instead, I describe it as a transformation not only because the author of the short story also wrote the filmscript, but also because the film itself displays an awareness of its medial potentials and limitations (framing, cutting, camera movements, stills, etc.) that go beyond any simple presentation of a text on the screen. In this respect, it is significant that the opening credits do not mention the short story, but present the film as based upon "un scénario original de Gabriel García Márquez."[11]

The first image of the film shows the black letter "A" on a white surface. As the camera zooms out, more and more letters appear, until the screen shows two tombstones with the written names "AMADÍS EL GRANDE" and "AMADÍS EL HIJO," surrounded by a wasteland of sand, pebbles, and rocks. The shot is accompanied by the sound of wind and of clinking glass. The camera then portrays the white, stony ground next to the gravestones.

The structure slowly changes. When the camera zooms out again, the audience discovers that the grains are no longer pebbles in the dust, but soap bubbles in a bathtub. While a voice off-camera narrates "la abuela se estaba bañando," the surface of the bubbles begins to move and bulge, and the back of a woman surfaces from below. It is the grandmother's back, with a large tattoo on it. The image is Guerra's intermedial translation of García Márquez's initial description of the grandmother, who is compared with a "ballena blanca… [con] el hombro potente tatuado" (97). This early sequence already presents the two main *atopic* sites of the short story, the desert and the sea. The stony ground gradually changes into bubbles over water, and it is only after the camera has zoomed out of the different surroundings (the desert with the tombstones in the first and the bathroom in the second shot) that the viewers discover the alternation. Guerra uses a succession of close-ups on structurally similar surfaces to create the first spatial metamorphose of the film. The opposed places of the dusty soil and of water become indistinct as a result of the focus on their structural similarities. Through the juxtaposition, the scene of the two dead men, buried in the dust, and the presentation of the grandmother, emerging from under water, can be interpreted in relation to each other: The woman might be a perpetuator of the system of exploitation, or even the reincarnation of the former masters.

The next scenes show the interior of the grandmother's over-ornamented house with statuettes, mirrors, portraits, antique furniture, crystal chandeliers, oriental rugs, and velvet draperies. Guerra's presentation of this treasure chamber, filled with the mementoes of the past, is a visual translation of the description in García Márquez's short story into the filmic medium. The text is composed of long sentences with numerous attributes, adjectives and subordinate clauses with rich interior rhymes, such as "la casa… era oscura y abigarrada, con muebles frenéticos… y arañas de lágrimas y ángeles de alabastro" (98). It also verbally mentions the otherness of "aquel refugio incomprensible… lejos de todo, en el alma del desierto" (98–99). The film camera slowly moves over details of the objects of this bizarre abundance. Sometimes it zooms in on them to such a degree that the viewers are unable to identify them (such as a single piece of a crystal chandelier or the fold of a curtain). In addition to these too close-up shots, the camera is positioned high above the ceiling, presenting the room as a huge container of indistinguishable objects. Both camera positions run counter to filmic viewing habits. Either too close or too distant from the objects, the film lens presents the materiality of the things as a visually overwhelming mass.

The text's semantic and syntactic richness, and the film's visual abundance, convey the grandmother's *horror vacui.* This anxiety is twofold: on the one hand, the profusion of objects is the product of her "horror" to face the possible "void" of her own, solitary life; on the other hand, it is the result of her fight against the surrounding "void" of the desert.[12] In the film, even more than in the text, the house becomes the site of an obsessive creating, inscribing, and cultivating of the grandmother's individual traits in the *atopic* and inhuman space. She is shown playing the grand piano, singing a melancholic song about the loss of her virginity, with the ostrich looking into the room from outside the window.[13] She is sobbing, while listening to old musical pieces on the gramophone. At night, although already asleep, she gives Eréndira a long list of orders to perpetuate the site of the cult of her self, to which the granddaughter only responds with a docile "sí, abuela," while she sleepwalks through the house. But the wind of change has already infiltrated the house and makes the objects move according to its will. As it increases, the glass pieces tinkle, the fabrics and fringes move, the chandelier falls down, and the flames set the curtains on fire.

After the house has burned down, the first trading of the "good" Eréndira takes place in a gloomy shop. Under a torrential rain, the man takes the girl out to his hut behind the shop. When she attempts to escape, he violently slaps her face. Here, the film changes to slow motion, and shows her falling body as if it were slowly floating under water. This technical slowdown visualizes the literary description of the girl's mental evasion to a different space-time. Her practice of manipulating space has altered with this shock experience. While she is raped, she passively lies in the hammock, with her gaze lost in space. Guerra alludes to an alternative space within the present site of suppression through changing viewpoints and a string of aquatic metaphors. The camera now shows two alternating sets of images: it focuses on parts of her naked body from above (her breasts, chin, shoulders, and hair). Here, the viewers are sharing the voyeuristic gaze with the rapist. Then, the camera shows close-ups of Eréndira's eyes and images of scraps of cloths in different colors. This second point of view presents the girl's inner vision. It is the visual transformation of García Márquez's description, "se quedó como fascinada con las franjas de luna de un pescado que pasó navegando en el aire de la tormenta" (105). The described fish, flying in the moonbeams of the storm, is now shown as a piece of cloth in the form of a fish, with stitched scales in pearly and blue colors. This cloth flaps in the air and has a hypnotizing power over the girl, who mentally unites with the freely floating object. With a stronger suggestive power than in the short story, this sequence in the film introduces the radically other space beyond subjugation, which will become the protagonist's non-space at the end of the film.

The grandmother and Eréndira embark on their travels, together with numerous remnants of the house, including the two coffins of the Amadises and a life-size marble statue. A shabby truck drives through a dusty and stony desert of no distinguishable features, and seems to stop randomly at a place that looks identical to the ones the travelers have just passed through. As soon as the tent is erected, the grandmother sits down on her throne. A man with a pack-donkey approaches (see fig. 7.1). He is the postman, and more precisely for regular mail and not for airmail, as he notes immediately after the grandmother has named

Fig. 7.1. Scene from *Eréndira* (dir. Ruy Guerra, Les Films du Triangle, 1982). The grandmother, on her throne, points the postman to Eréndira's tent.

the price of Eréndira's services. He gets a discount, and is asked by the procuress in return to spread the word about the young prostitute. The viewers possibly wonder where this character might have come from and where he is about to go in the vastness of sand, stones, and changing horizons. The film does not explain his sudden appearance, as it will not elucidate similar actions of characters in the following episodes. Guerra's *Eréndira* presents an environment far beyond everyday experience and logics, similar to a magical, oneiric, or surrealist state. This extraordinary ambiance is intensified through the sharp contrast with the depiction of brutality and poverty as elements in the tradition of the Italian neorealist cinema and the Brazilian *Cinema Novo* with their clear impetus to realistically portray the brutality of life and gloomy economic and social situations.

The next forty-five minutes of the film show Eréndira at different sites, surrounded by an increasing number of men waiting for her, as well as an increasingly satisfied grandmother, who spends her days counting money and her nights recounting her own grandeur and fame as a prostitute. The film directly juxtaposes the grandmother's deliriums with the granddaughter's suffering. For instance in the scene when Ulises sneaks into the tent, and tries to convince the exhausted girl to make love, the grandmother hallucinates about her first meeting with Amadís el Grande, and about their immediate attraction to each other.

The two beds are separated by a diaphanous veil. Both women repeatedly observe each other (Eréndira is awake, while the old woman looks over to her in her sleep). The analogous settings bring forward the presentation of Eréndira's fate as the reiteration of the grandmother's life story, an aspect of the relation between the two women that was less explicit in the literary text. The two are separated by a thin veil and by some fifty years. Repetition, in this context, is yet another element that promotes the disquieting *horror vacui* among the characters and within each of them. The grandmother clearly does not want her granddaughter to imitate her, since this would be a mere repetition of her sameness. Instead, she forces Eréndira to surpass her: She describes herself as "la dama," but wants Eréndira to be "una reina." However, this rhetoric of outdoing only stresses the repetition, since neither she nor her grandchild reaches these goals.

The film shows Eréndira's course toward an "amor vacui" as a chain of passages through multiple sites of repression, with the bed as their *pars pro toto*. The presentations of beds from a wide array of angles and perspectives stress the significance of the place as the microcosm of Eréndira's individual sufferings, and of the economic prosperity the "good" Eréndira provides for her grandmother. Many shots contrast the limitedness of the beds with sites that convey a radical spatial openness, such as a take when the car is driving through places of no distinguishable features, or a scene that shows Eréndira in front of a sheer white wall and floor in the convent, or the final shot of her escape into the pure openness of the desert. Guerra presents the duality of spaces of individuality (the sites of Eréndira's personal exploitation and the few allusions to her pleasures, and the grandmother's delirium) with sites of non-individuality (the darkness of the night, the white wall in the cloister, the sand dunes in the desert).

After the encounter with the missionaries, the next phase of the prostitute's migration brings her to the bed of a senator. Here, the film borrows from García Márquez's short story "Muerte más allá del amor" ("Death Constant beyond Love"), included in the same collection as the text on Eréndira. Just as the senator's campaign for re-election is a huge staging (he is speaking in front of a cheaply painted wall made of cardboard), his bedroom is an arrangement of clichés of a powerful man's resting place. He remarks how much he hates the falseness around him, and also tells her about his insuperable loneliness, which he feels to be equal to hers. He then names the day and time of his death. The inclusion of this special client in the cinematographic narration is a clear statement on the demagogical control of "staging" as a political praxis. On the intradiegetic level, it emphasizes Eréndira's success with men of all classes and backgrounds and underscores the importance of the theme of solitude. Guerra's film also shows the senator's end: He dies in the back seat of his car, whispering Eréndira's name. As the car moves away from the camera, it suddenly disappears in the dust, without leaving any trace. In contrast to the initial shot with the two majestic tombstones in the desert, the lone senator's death is presented as a vanishing pulverization. This scene foreshadows the ending of the protagonist, who will also disappear without leaving a trace in space.

The film accentuates the difference between Eréndira's passivity and all its other characters' collective practice of space, such as the angry prostitutes or Eréndira's customers. While the men are waiting to take their turns, they "inscribe" themselves in space: The camera moves along the seemingly endless line of men standing in front of the tent, of shops, stands, and stalls at the fairground and on the pedestrian walks in the town. Theirs is a social use of space. Except for Eréndira, who is filmed chained to her bed on the main square from a top view shot, all characters in this sequence are portrayed from about eye-level. With the exception of the protagonist, everyone has a shadow. The characters' physical corporeality covers the ground and casts shadows. Eréndira's corporeal reaction to space is again different from all the others' performances. I read her character, from this sequence on and during the subsequent final ten minutes of the film, as a being beyond the life-dead duality, of a radically singular corporeality and therefore practice of space. In her deep solitude, Eréndira neither interacts with others, nor reacts to physical space in any way. She has no shadow, and in the end will not even leave a trace, free from the laws of gravity.

One of the final sites that the film shows is the seashore, with the tent in the middle of a long beach. It is in the interstice between the desert and the sea where the grandmother dies and where Eréndira progresses to a radically different state. The interior of the tent is similar to the interior of the grandmother's house at the beginning of the film. The over-abundance of objects again indicates her *horror vacui*. During Ulises's numerous attempts to kill the grandmother, Eréndira is passive. It is not until the moment when the dead grandmother and Eréndira's exhausted lover lie on the ground that she becomes active. Without hesitation, she turns away from the two beings to whom she has had the closest relationship in her life, and runs out of the tent, across the beach, to the dunes. The camera shows her back, from Ulises's point of view. As she disappears in the distance, her voice off camera says: "Iba corriendo contra el viento, más veloz que un venado, y ninguna voz de ese mundo me podía detener." She does not leave footprints. At the spots that her feet have touched appear red rose blossoms (see fig. 7.2). After a few seconds, the spots again take on a sandy color. A strong wind is blowing. The final shot of the film shows the dunes without any trace of her.

The endings in the text and film are similar, except for Guerra's inclusion of the rose blossoms and the changing of a single per-

Fig. 7.2. Final shot from Guerra's *Eréndira.* The protagonist vanishes into the void. Her footprints become red rose blossoms (dir. Ruy Guerra, Les Films du Triangle, 1982).

sonal pronoun: In the short story it is the narrator who says that no voice in the world could stop her ("la podía detener"). In the film, Eréndira speaks for herself ("me podía detener"). As she runs away, she breaks her silence and pronounces her liberty from the forced exploitation she has suffered throughout her existence. The ending of the film intensifies the concept of radical openness that has been described in the text. Guerra uses a variety of props and cinematographic devices that all convey the idea of a radically *atopic* "beyond." The camera remains in a fixed position, while Eréndira runs out of focus. Her farewell to the audience comes from an indeterminate space: since her body has disappeared, her voice is literally "off" the scene. After the disappearance of the body, and the voluntary silencing of the voice, the viewers are left with an uninhabited, inhuman landscape. The sound of the wind and the rasping sand remind them that the shapes of the dunes are only momentary. The character and her voice have dispersed in a space that is shown to be inscrutable and merely transitory.

The concluding scene of the film also presents a creative imagining on how to surpass the very structures of (imperial, colonial, generic, or spatial) suppression. At the beginning of this chapter,

I described Eréndira as a subaltern being, following Spivak's concept. However, at the very end of the film she speaks. Another of Spivak's essays helps me to interpret this utterance as a speech act that can undo the very hegemony of discourse. In "Echo" (1993), Spivak re-reads the deaths of the figures of Narcissus and Echo in Ovid's *Metamorphoses*:

> At the moment of Narcissus' death, his sisters come to mourn him and in the place of the body find the flower. The body seems to have been inscribed into nature… By contrast Echo's echoing farewell comes from a space already insufficiently inscribed… Her desire and performance are dispensed into absolute chance rather than an obstinate choice, as in the case of Narcissus… the lithography of Echo's bony remains merely points out to the risk of response. (*The Spivak Reader* 184–85)

Guerra's protagonist unifies characteristics of both mythical figures: For a few seconds, the place of the body is covered with flowers, as in the Narcissus story. The rose blossoms inscribe Eréndira's fate in space and create a monument to her life, just like any floral arrangement on a tombstone. But her farewell is also similar to Echo's, since it is enunciated from an indistinct and moving *atopos* that precisely annihilates any inscription in space. Guerra's Eréndira does not leave a reminder, such as the metamorphosed daffodil or Echo's metonymical, resounding voice in space. The former subaltern actively chooses not to speak to and about the oppressor and does not affirm authority, according to the former hierarchy, through her own voice. Her last utterance and subsequent silencing allude to a transition toward an indefinable site beyond common spatiality. The body and voice have left the screen and abandoned the very concepts of subjugation and dominance. While García Márquez plays with alternative cultural propensities toward space and belonging, the ending in Guerra's film proposes a concept of radical openness where dispersion has ceased to be a negative term.

Epilogue

The Non-Space Revisited

It is challenging to approach the spaces in texts and films—slowly and with many detours via scarce, indirect descriptions and by way of the characters' reactions toward their surroundings. One has to read "against the grain" and detect, not a prominent textual or filmic element, but on the contrary, a discrete and almost invisible entity, at least at first sight. The scant portrayals of space initially delude the characters, who fail to notice the impact of this force in their life-worlds. The spaces expose their occupants to equivocality; the shock the characters experience when facing slippery, dark, or merging sites provokes a heightened sense of spatial awareness, which implies a revision of taken-for granted concepts of subjectivity and self-positioning in a social context.

In literature and film, detailed descriptions generally foster a process of reification with the work of art, where the readers and viewers follow the textual and filmic indications and become figuratively drawn into the fictional worlds. The authors and directors I studied proceeded in an inverse fashion by transmitting blank spots and fleeting sites that defy spatial conventions of a real *topos* or a projected *u-* or *dystopos*. Likewise, the spaces are too vague to be metaphors for clearly definable extratextual and extrafilmic concepts. The de-naturalizing strategy of presenting non-spaces of instability and slipperiness may provoke a bewilderment in the readers and viewers that is similar to the characters' spatial disquiet. The spaces in suspense point toward their creators' search for ways out of epistemic dichotomies, and venture to re-think established concepts of space, ground, and demarcation.

Such artistic impetus or "voluntad de no definir…, [de] apunta[r] a un territorio ambiguo, del que [los personajes] son los pobres y mezquinos profetas," as Julio Cortázar describes it in a letter to Manuel Antin (*Cartas 1937–1963* 503), parallels the poststructuralist notions of deferral or *différance*. I agree with Carlos Alonso, who reads Cortázar's writings as a "coeval and sui generis exploration of issues that preoccupied thinkers such as Derrida, Lacan, Serres and several others" (14). I hope to have shown that not only Cortázar, but several other writers of the *nueva narrativa* movement as well as directors of their filmic translations explore such spaces of suspension and propose an epistemological and cognitive broadening of spatial concepts. For Michel Foucault,

> la littérature, ce n'est pas le langage se rapprochant de soi jusqu'au point de sa brûlante manifestation, c'est le langage se mettant au plus loin de lui-même, et si, en cette mise "hors de soi," il dévoile son être propre, cette clarté soudaine révèle un écart plutôt qu'un repli, une dispersion plutôt qu'un retour des signes sur eux-mêmes. (...) L'espace de cette pensée... [c'est] l'invincible absence... le vide... la distance..., —cette pensée... par rapport à la positivité de notre savoir, constitue ce qu'on pourrait appeler d'un mot "la pensée du dehors." (Foucault and Blanchot 13, 16)

In light of the texts analyzed in the previous chapters, it is clear that not only literature, but also film can be the medium of such thinking, imagining, and viewing of alternative spaces beyond the everyday perception of the three-dimensional life-world. What is more, through the lens of the cinematographic medium, the textual "space-fictions" reveal themselves further. Both media, in the process of transformation, translation, adaptation, or metamorphosis, illuminate each other in the challenging endeavor to capture or indirectly allude to the disquieting sites of echoes, gaps, absences, and radical openness. The intermedial approach, with its necessary focuses on the "third" space between media, helps to grasp the elusive phenomenon of space in the short fiction and films, yet without curtailing its spatial and narrative characteristics.

An unexpected discovery in this study of the forms of spatial consciousness in literature and film was the impact of sound. The street corners and stages in Borges's short stories and their transformations to the screen, the juxtaposed sites in "Cartas de mamá" and the two films inspired by the text, the world of Comala in the novella and the two films, all are pervaded by sounds and echoes from different time-spaces. The bodiless, transparent, and moving medium circumscribes the radical and slippery spaces in a paradigmatic way. Sound waves necessarily need a barrier—a wall or the human eardrum—to resonate and be perceived. Through the echoing, the sonic device indirectly alludes to space, and since it is able even to penetrate complete darkness and go around corners, it can open up sites out of our sight, beyond the described, imagined, or shown surroundings (Leyshon, Matless, and Revill 1–7).

In lieu of a finalizing conclusion, which would run counter to the object of study of active and slippery spaces conveyed in text and a visual media, I wish to end with an intermedial excursus. In the lithography *Print Gallery*, M.C. Escher shows on the left a man in a gallery, looking at a work of art (see fig. 8). The painting he is contemplating has a frame on its left side. The right side,

Fig. 8. *Print Gallery* (M.C. Escher, 1956, Lithograph). Rpt. with permission of the M.C. Escher Company.

however, has no margin. In the painting, the man is looking at the roof of a building that arches over until it becomes the roof of one of the arcades of the print gallery, the (painted) observer's space. The artistic world has entered his world. Furthermore, a woman, peering out of a window within the painting that the (painted) character is looking at, is looking back at him. The represented outside space and the represented artistic space intertwine as in a Moebius strip in mutual and inextricable contemplation. In glancing at each other's worlds, the characters reflect on the relativities and blurring margins of the representation in front of them, and also on their own realities. The contemplation of representation leads to self-reflection. According to Mieke Bal, such a depiction of self-reflection through the contemplation of the other, "proposes a radical view of the world as itself is constructed, which entails a critical perspective on the world and its changeability" (*Reading "Rembrandt"* 257). Similar to the texts and films I studied in the previous chapters, Escher's lithography is a meditation on the merging perspectives and, in a broader sense, on the changeability of the fictive worlds on the canvas (the site of the gallery and the site of the painted scene at a seaside). The gradual blurring of the artistic framing and the stable surroundings of the gallery become "metavisual" signs for the observers. The figures are looking beyond their own worlds, and thus discern an additional reality outside the multiple frames on the canvas. A possible metanarrative reality outside the margin of the lithography is the world of the observers of these two observers. Like the characters on the canvas, we are invited to contemplate our realities and meditate on their changeability, relativity, and thereby discover the constructed, possibly volatile features of them.

Escher includes another element to foster such a meditation: The center of his painting, showing a print gallery, which has the title *Print Gallery*, is a void white spot. The picture of multiple representations of artistic spaces displays in its center a non-space, marked by an absence, which is the artist's signature. As the observers, readers, viewers, listeners of works of art we are invited not to overlook the open spot, but to bear the void, and to actively participate in the making of the work of art by "filling in the blank." The void in the center of Escher's painting expounds on the problem of the status of artistic and extra-artistic space, and, indirectly, on the conception of the self in the world. In the same way as the intradiegetic characters in *Print Gallery*, albeit not always as serene as they are, the characters in the short narratives and films I have analyzed are forced to reckon with their spaces, since they realize that they cannot establish a distance toward them, but are standing in the middle of them, are part of them, and have to rebuild, invent, and assume them with every new step.

Notes

Preface
Approaching Un-common Grounds

1. Examples would be Carlos Onetti's *El pozo* (*The Pit*) [1939], *Para una tumba sin nombre* (*A Grave with No Name*) [1959], and *El astillero* (*The Shipyard*) [1961], José Donoso's *El lugar sin límites* (*The Place without Limits*) [1966], or Carlos Fuentes's *Zona sagrada* (*Sacred Zone*) [1967].

2. Among the cinematic translations of "non-spaces," described in literary texts, are Arturo Ripstein's *El lugar sin límites* [1977], based on the homonymous novel by José Donoso [1966]; and many filmic translations of Cortázar's short stories, such as Manuel Antin's *Circe* [1962] based on Cortázar's text of the same name (*Bestiario, Bestiary*) [1951] and Antin's *Intimidad de los parques* (*Intimity of Parks*) [1964] inspired by the two Cortázar stories "Continuidad del los parques" ("Continuity of Parks") and "El ídolo de las Cícladas" ("The Idol of the Cyclades"), both from *Final del juego* (*End of the Game*) [1956]; furthermore, Luigi Comencini's *L'ingorgo (una storia impossibile)* ("Traffic Jam [An Impossible Story]) [1978] and Jean-Luc Godard's *Week-end* [1967], both free adaptations of Cortázar's "La autopista del sur" ("The Southern Thruway") from *Todos los fuegos el fuego* (*All the Fires the Fire*) [1966]. Several more recent cinematographic examples of portrayals of spaces of disquiet inspired by Cortázar's short stories are Robert Cerendelli's *Instrucciones para subir una escalera* (*Instructions to Climb a Staircase*) [1999] on the short text of the same name; Alexandre Aja's *Furia* (*Fury*) [1999] on Cortázar's "Graffiti" (*Queremos tanto a Glenda, We Love Glenda so Much)* [1980]; Zhanna Kleimann's *Fear of Alternative Realities* [1999] and Harriet Marin's *La nuit face au ciel* (*The Night Face Up*) [1999], both based on Cortázar's "La noche boca arriba" ("The Night Face Up," *Final del juego*) [1956]; and finally Roberto Gervitz's *Jogo subterrâneo* (Underground Game) [2005] inspired by Cortázar's "Manuscrito hallado en un bolsillo" ("Manuscript Found in a Pocket") from *Octaedro* (*Octaeder*) [1974]. Several free adaptations of García Márquez's writings, such as Fernando Birri's *Un señor muy viejo con unas alas enormes* (*A Very Old Man with Enormous Wings*) [1988], Arturo Ripstein's *El coronel no tiene quien le escriba* (*No One Writes to the Colonel*) [1998], and Ruy Guerra's *In Evil Hour* on García Márquez's *La mala hora* (*In Evil Hour*) [2004] also display puzzling universes that unsettle their users, readers, and viewers, as a result of their elusiveness and changeability.

Introduction:
Spotting the Non-Space

1. Two epistemological changes altered the perception of space in the twentieth century to a great extent: The modification from the Euclidian conception of space to the one outlined in Einstein's General Theory of Relativity, which is described to be curved and gravitational, therefore largely determined by a distribution of masses, and the assumption, initiated by Georges Lemaître and developed by Edwin Hubble, that space is not only infinite, but expanding. For a detailed analysis of the new perceptions and theories of space from the point of view of physics, mathematics, and cosmological studies, see Salomon Bochner's entry on "space" in the *Dictionary of the History of Ideas.*

2. I understand the notion of a text in a poststructuralist way, where a text designates a site for the production and proliferation of meaning through the use of distinctive words and sentences.

3. See Wolfgang Iser: "The Reading Process: A Phenomenological Approach," in *Reader-Response Criticism: From Formalism to Post-Structuralism*: "The phenomenological theory of art lays full stress on the idea that, in considering a literary work, one must take into account not only the actual text, but also, and in equal measure, the actions involved in responding to that text… The text as such offers different 'schematised views' through which the subject matter of the work can come to light, but the actual bringing to light is an action of 'Konkretisation'… The literary work cannot be completely identical with the text, or with the realization of the text, but in fact must lie halfway between the two… It is the virtuality of the work that gives rise to its dynamic nature, and this in turn is the precondition for the effects that the work calls forth… Reading causes the literary work to unfold its inherent dynamic character" (50–51).

4. The concept of interpretation is much discussed in recent theoretic discourse. It has been accused of being too vague and unreliable, because of the subjectivity it involves. I do not see subjectivity to be negative or harmful. On the contrary, I support its necessity in theory. I concur with Mieke Bal's statement from the introduction to *"Reading" Rembrandt*: "I subscribe to the general skepticism concerning the possibility of circumscribing meaning, but… I do not find interpretation futile… Interpretation [is] as important, as valuable, as writing and painting… While I find much that is intellectually attractive in the currently widespread resistance to interpretation presented in response to the recognition of the free play of signs and meanings, I also see it as a renewed threat to the freedom of cultural participation, a new form of censorship… censorship *of* interpretation can be used to conceal the censorship *by* interpretation. That is why the resistance to interpretation can receive such wide acclaim, from progressive as well as from conservative ideologues" (13–14).

5. Many modern artists directly challenge the conventions of spatiality. Paul Cézanne is probably the first Western painter who does not attempt to represent an outside space, but to present an interior personal spatial layout. At the beginning of the twentieth century, the Cubist artists radically deconstruct the convention of the central perspective in art, and present instead a plurality of points of view within a painting or collage. Pablo Picasso, Hans Arp, and Wassily Kandinsky painted surfaces that challenge our traditional conception of space, based on a single vanishing point. Mark Rothko, among other abstract artists, presented in his *Color Field* paintings compositions of undiluted colors dialoguing with each other, without any outline of a three-dimensional setting.

6. All these devices do not exclusively belong to the cinematic practice, but to all visual arts. They form part of a convention, created for Renaissance painting, which, according to Salomon Bochner, "was intended to secure a two-dimensional mimetic illusion of three dimensional actuality... the central structural device for achieving this way was the introduction of a 'vanishing point' at infinity" (302).

7. Benjamin Jowett, in his introduction to the text, underscores that "Plato may be regarded as the 'captain' ('arhchegoz') or leader of a goodly band of followers; for in the *Republic* is to be found the original of Cicero's *De Republica*, of St. Augustine's *City of God*, of the *Utopia* of Sir Thomas More, and of the numerous other imaginary states which are framed upon the same model... [It] is also the first treatise upon education, of which the writings of Milton and Locke, Rousseau, Jean Paul, and Goethe are the legitimate descendants. Like Dante..., [Plato] has a revelation of another life; like Bacon, he is profoundly impressed with the unity of knowledge. ... He is the father of idealism in philosophy, in politics, in literature. And many of the latest conceptions of modern thinkers and statesmen, such as the unity of knowledge, the reign of law, and the equality of the sexes, have been anticipated in a dream by him" (no pagination). <http://classics.mit.edu/Plato/republic.1.introduction.html>.

8. Augé did not use the French term *supermodernité* (the prefix exists in French, although as an Anglicism), but instead *surmodernité*, probably to echo another concept that intended to transcend an apparently fixed axiom, the *sur-réalisme*. This possible connotation gets lost in the translation.

9. Augé uses the term *demeure* to describe this anthropological space of individual and social identification. This term has no English equivalent.

10. I thank one of the reviewers of my manuscript for this terminological suggestion.

11. However, I do not suggest that the designed spaces condition or predispose the characters' fate. Such an argument does not take into account the works' status as artistic and artificial, individual elaborations.

12. The argument of fidelity is especially strong when modernist texts serve as models for films. One might think about the controversial discussions on Orson Welles's and David Hugh Jones's cinematic adaptations of Franz Kafka's *The Trial* or about Volker Schlöndorff's *A Love of Swann* and Raoul Ruiz's *Time Regained*, based on novels by Marcel Proust, or Vladimir Nabokov's *Lolita* and Stanley Kubrick's adaptation, for which Nabokov wrote the screenplay.

13. For a definition of intertextuality, I follow Julia Kristeva's concept, elaborated in *Le texte du roman*. Kristeva defines any text, "comme un appareil translinguistique qui redistribue l'ordre de la langue, en mettant en relation une parole communicative... avec différents types d'énoncés antérieurs ou synchroniques. Un texte est donc une productivité, ce qui veut dire: (1) son rapport à la langue dans laquelle il se situe est redistributif (destructifconstructiv)... (2) il est une permutation de textes, une inter-textualité: dans l'espace d'un texte plusieurs énoncés, pris d'autres textes, se croisent" (12).

14. For further analyses on intermediality in Hispanic literature and film, see *Kino-(Ro)Mania—Intermedialität zwischen Film und Literatur*, edited by Jochen Mecke and Volker Roloff; Sylvia Kling's *Filmologie und Intermedialität—Der filmologische Beitrag zu einem aktuellen medienwissenschaftlichen Konzept*; Joachim Paech's essay "Artwork-Text-Medium: Steps en Route to Intermediality"; and *Literatur intermedial. Musik, Malerei, Photographie, Film*, edited by Peter V. Zima.

15. See the definition of the term in the *Oxford English Dictionary* or in the German Dictionary *Medientheorie. Medienwissenschaft*, edited by Helmut Schanze. According to Schanze, the field of "intermedial comparative studies" ("Medienkomparatistik") comprehends the comparative studies. Both approaches are intercultural and transnational. But whereas the older concept is based mainly on the analysis of literary texts, an intermedial study analyzes in a more integrative way manifold enunciations from different media. "Within the scope of a study of literature, communication, art or of general media studies, the intermedial comparative approach abolishes the former differentiation of single enunciations and searches for the superior concept of an integrative cultural understanding of medial acts" (224; my translation).

16. For an analysis of the impact of Bakhtin's concept in intermedial studies, see Rolf Kloepfer's article "Intertextualität und Intermedialität oder die Rückkehr zum dialogischen Prinzip. Bachtins Theoreme als Grundlage für Literatur- und Filmtheorie" in *Kino-(Ro)Mania—Intermedialität zwischen Film und Literatur* (23–46).

17. José Ortega y Gasset, in his cardinal essay "La deshumanización del arte" from 1925, was probably one of the first to underline this difficulty. He distinguishes between two mutually exclusive ways of looking at a work of art. Giving the example of a garden, seen through a window, he points out toward, on the one hand, an optic centered in the object (the trees, paths, flowers in the garden) and, on the other hand, an optic focusing on the medium itself (the glass of the window, the crossbar, dividing the scene, the vertical and horizontal axes). It is this second mode of perception that, according to Ortega y Gasset, procures aesthetic delight (*La deshumanización del arte y otros ensayos de estética* 17).

18. Although Derrida's investigations in media's conditions, especially his concept of deferral, are clear models for the theorists, the influence of his thought is scarcely mentioned in the theoretical approaches to intermediality. The only investigation on the impact of Derrida's thought in current media-philosophy I could find is Christoph Ernst's "Gespenst, Phantom, Wiedergänger. Zur medienphilosophischen Lektüre der Dekonstruktion" in *Perspektiven interdisziplinärer Medienphilosophie*. Referring to Derrida's work *Le spectre de Marx*, Ernst argues that the medial operation, for the French theorist, is a space of transference outside established temporal and spatial reference: "a space of transference… a-chronological and a-topic" (56; my translation).

Chapter One
Into Spatial Vagueness: Jorge Luis Borges's and Miguel Picaso's *Hombre de la esquina rosada*

1. Edgardo Cozarinsky's *Borges in/and/on Film* is the first of the subject matter (1988), followed by María Martínez Andrade's "Espacio e identidad en tres relatos de Borges" (2001). Sophia Psarra's "'The Book and the Labyrinth Were One and the Same'—Narrative and Architecture in Borges' Fictions" (2003) proposes a formal reading of the role of architecture in three short stories and points out that the texts are based on a tension between the linear progression of the story and the underlying symmetrical structure that organizes all narrative elements. In the context of the function of deictic utterances and their emphasis on "situatedness," see Bill Richardson's "Spatial and Deictic Reference in Three Borges Stories" (1999). Nataly Tcherepashenets's comparative *Place and Displacement in the Narrative World of Jorge Luis Borges and Julio Cortázar* (2008) focuses on Borges's ironic challenging of the concept of place as revelation and the underlying questioning of place as a trope that stands for the human aspiration to bridge the gap between the finite and the infinite. Arturo Echavarría's "El arte de la jardinería china: 'El jardín de los senderos que se bifurcan'" (*El arte de la jardinería china en Borges y otros estudios,* 2006) is a study of Borges's reinterpretation of the symbol of the Chinese garden, a carefully arranged world in miniature, which only seems to be chaotic and endless, as an emblem for his own theory of writing and interpreting.

2. The importance of the theme of cartography in Borges might be one of the reasons for the attraction of his fiction for geographical research. As James Corner, in "The Agency of Mapping: Speculation, Critique and Invention" notes: "Jorge Luis Borges' tale of a fully detailed and life-sized map that eventually tore and weathered to shreds across the actual territory it covered is frequently quoted in essays on mapping. Not only does the tale beautifully capture the cartographic imagination, it goes to the heart of a tension between reality and representation, between the territory and the map. … Not only is the map an inferior, secondary representation of territory but the more detailed and life-like the map strives to be, the more redundant… it becomes" (221).

3. There are many analyses of the metaphor of the labyrinth in Borges's short stories. Among them, John Barth, in "The Literature of Exhaustion," refers to the labyrinth's characteristic as a place of possibilities: "A labyrinth, after all, is a place in which, ideally, all the possibilities of choice (of direction, in this case) are embodied, and… must be exhausted before one reaches the heart" (34). Saúl Yurkiévich, in "Nueva refutación del cosmos" highlights the variety of the labyrinths and their artificiality: "El laberinto humano es una transición: laberintos espaciales como la casa de Asterión… laberintos de escaleras… laberintos espejados… laberintos temporales, textuales, discursivos… laberintos eventuales… progresivos… laberintos cosmológicos como Tlön. Todos son artificios concebidos por hombres para desorientar a otros hombres, destinados a que los hombres los descifren" (4).

4. The English word *corner* has two translations in Spanish: "rincón" (a corner in a room, an obtuse angle) and "esquina" (a street corner, an acute angle). The narrator does not encounter the *esquina*, mentioned in the title. But he is trapped in a *rincón*, and feels humiliated by its narrowness.

5. Borges's short story was also adapted in 1962, by the Argentinean director René Mugica (*Hombre de la esquina rosada*, 70 minutes, an Argentina Sono Film production). Picazo presents a much more meditated and artistic version than Mugica; therefore, I will only analyze his film. For descriptions of Picazo's filmography see Thomas G. Deveny's *Contemporary Spanish Film from Fiction* and entries on his work in the *Diccionario del cine español*, edited by José Luis Borau.

6. There is no reference to the poem, being a text by Borges, in the film or in the epilogue.

7. The voice starts reciting at the beginning of the film, when the camera shows Lujanera. It goes on for more than four minutes.

Chapter Two
The Power of Staging: Spaces of Emulation in Jorge Luis Borges's "Tema del traidor y del héroe" and Bernardo Bertolucci's *Strategia del ragno*

1. Lisa Block de Behar refers to this short story to illustrate Borges's generally short and sparse descriptions of spaces in his texts: "Only infrequently, in his writings, did Borges describe the space in which the actions of his stories took place. … One of his recourses of universalization consists of the decircumstantialization of episodes, opting, precisely, not to mention the places that are no more than accidents of universal space… an… example of decircumstantialization—a globalization *avant la lettre*—[is] 'Theme of the Traitor and the Hero'" (66–67).

2. Sophia Psarra notes that the choice of Dublin as the setting can be read as an intertextual reference to the city in James Joyce's *Ulysses*, and, in a broader sense, to the literary *topos* of the city as labyrinth.

3. A sealed letter, found in the dead hero's pocket, warning him not to go to the theater that night, is echoing Shakespeare's *Julius Caesar*. Nolan's story also evokes a scene from *Macbeth*, when a beggar is speaking to Kilpatrick on the day of his death.

4. In the late 1940s, a few literary magazines in the United States and Europe had printed translations of isolated texts by the Argentinean author. His name started to appear in the European context with the French publications of *Fictions* (*idem)* in 1951, followed by *Labyrinthes* (*Labyrinths*) in 1953, *Enquêtes* (*Other Inquisitions*) in 1957, *Histoire de l'infamie* (*A Universal History of Infamy*) and *Histoire de l'éternité* (*A History of Eternity*) in 1958 (Cozarinsky 77–86).

5. Ollier paraphrases the beginning of the short story, when referring to the film he had seen a few years earlier: "The work was long and dense, woven from multiple episodes. … Perhaps I have forgotten some points… Peripheral sections of the story undoubtedly escape my memory. Today, May 13, 1963, I recall it this way: The action takes place in a stubborn, warlike country: Finland, Cuba, some capital coveted by the free world… let's say, Paris. Let's say 1958" (Cozarinsky 81).

6. My translation; the translations of the dialogues in the film, and initial and final credits are mine.

7. To distinguish the two homonymous characters, I will henceforth call the son "Athos Jr." and the father "Athos Sr."

8. The opera, similar to the short story by Borges and similar to the film it is performed in, is about plotting, deception, and betrayal. The hunchback court jester Rigoletto plans to kill the Duke of Mantua. The initial plot of the conspirators in *Strategia del ragno* is analogous to the storyline of the opera: Athos Sr. and his friends had planned to kill another "Duke," Mussolini (whose epithet was "il Duce"). *Rigoletto* can therefore be interpreted as a *palimpsest*, as yet another sub-text or source of inspiration for the film, along with Borges's short story (Fernández Ferrer 39–41).

9. In this respect, I disagree with Marta Acosta, who interprets the initial sequence as a "traditional tale-like beginning: the arrival of a train at a small-town station" (65). As I read it, this sequence does not evoke a tale, but refers to the artistic and technical beginning of cinematography.

10. I would like to thank Gustavo Pellón for this information.

11. Matteo provides a geographical and historical background of the place's harmonic architecture, chosen by Bertolucci: "Tara is the fictional name given to the real Renaissance city of Sabbioneta, where the movie was filmed, a town of about 5,000 inhabitants near the northern city of Parma, in the Po Valley. … Most of it was built over a period of only a few years, in the sixteenth century…, in accordance with the most current notions of architecture and urban planning. The result is a strikingly unadulterated Renaissance environment, with very few heterogeneous traces of previous or subsequent styles. The ensemble offers a feeling of purity and harmony" (21–22).

12. Bolongaro notes that the name Draifa, a feminization of the name Dreyfus, "points not only to the traitor/hero dichotomy, but also to the issue of the role of intellectuals in national political struggles" (79).

13. When the desparate Athos Jr. is waiting for the train to come, after several announcements that the train would arrive late, a voice from inside the station tells him that Tara is sometimes "forgotten" by the world around: "Succede che si dimenticano que esistiamo" ("Sometimes they forget that we exist")

14. Tara's population reflects this lack of evolution. The town is populated by old men, sexually ambiguous children, and rabbits.

15. The way the townspeople speak is reminiscent of a dramatic representation. They solemnly over-accentuate and recite their words, with exaggerated gestures.

16. "Domani, ho un treno" ("My train leaves tomorrow"); "Ho un treno alle nove" ("My train leaves at nine"); "Sono qui… vorrei non essere qui, ho un treno…" ("I am here… I wish I would not be here, my train leaves…").

17. In the film there are various allusions to frames and different settings in a work of art: In several shots, Bertolucci refers to pictures and paintings. He creates frames as intermedial evocations of, for instance, works by Giorgio de Chirico and René Magritte. According to Wicks, "Bertolucci composes some of his frames to evoke the early work of Giorgio de Chirico, whose sterile colonnaded streets, sliced by sharp shadows and cold sunlight, suggest some ominous mystery (see especially *Nostalgia of the Infinite*, 1913; *The Mystery and Melancholy of a Street*, 1914; and *Metaphysic Landscape*, 1929). Toward the end of the film there is a scene in the square with umbrella-holding men and women that evokes René Magritte's *Golconda* (1953)" (29).

18. See, for instance, Borges's short stories "El espejo de los enigmas" ("The Mirror of Enigmas," *Otras inquisiciones/Other Inquisitions*) [1952], "Los espejos velados" ("The Draped Mirrors," *El hacedor/The Maker*) [1960], and "Límites" ("Limits," *El hacedor*) [1960]; and the poems "Los espejos" ("Mirrors," *El hacedor*) and "Al espejo" ("To the Mirror," *El oro de los tigres*/The Gold of Tigers) [1972].

Chapter Three
Screening the Void: Julio Cortázar's "Cartas de mamá," and Manuel Antin's and Miguel Picazo's Filmic Translations

1. Besides composing short fiction, poems, novels, and multimedia works with texts and images, Cortázar also published critical essays on various authors (Keats, Rimbaud, Poe, Dostoevsky, Camus, Claudel, Ocampo, Paz, among others), literary movements (Surrealism and Existentialism), and literary genres and art forms (short stories, novels, films, and photography). He also worked as a translator. His translation of Edgar Allan Poe's collected short stories has become the standard reference of Poe's work in the Spanish-speaking world.

2. According to Alazraki, "los relatos de Cortázar… captan experiencias inéditas que desbordan el ámbito de la Biblioteca y corretean por la vida… enredándose en esa madeja que es el mundo, para volver al texto transparentadas por el envión de su catarsis" (7).

3. Paula Félix-Didier, in "Cortázar, cazador de crepúsculos," elaborates on Cortázar's affinities for the artistic and life-world concept of the Surrealists: "El concepto de lo 'maravilloso-cotidiano' concebido por el surrealismo… Cortázar [lo] vivía como moral anticonvencional y como juego permanente. Sus posturas políticas y su arte poético se configuran en la convicción de que la imaginación y el arte… nos enseñan a mirar, pensar y sentir de nuevo" (7).

4. For a concise study of Cortázar's writing in relation to the French surrealist movement (writing, painting and plastics), see Evelyn Picon Garfield's *¿Es Julio Cortázar un surrealista?*

5. Much of Cortázar's work on the subject of the instantaneous was written prior to the publication of Robbe-Grillet's novel. Cortázar has not been influenced by the *Nouveau Romanciers* as he has been by the Surrealists.

6. According to Marcy E. Schwartz, in her analysis of *Territorios*, "Cortázar Under Exposure: Photography and Fiction in the City," "the French capital functions as a contrapuntal urban force to delineate the photographers' and essayist's positions vis à vis their city subjects. His reminiscences of Buenos Aires, where he can permit himself the most intimate and personal perspective, are written and 'imagined' from afar in Europe... The narrative voice parallels the reader/spectator who looks in from the outside, temporarily present but not *there*" (119; emphasis in original).

7. Jaime Alazraki compares the structure of the novel, not to a photograph of several projections, but to a kaleidoscope of transitory visual images: "La lectura de *62* podría compararse a una multiplicidad de figuras calidoscópicas... en su dinámica volubilidad y diversidad... Londres, Viena, París forman un prisma de espejos" (239–40).

8. The description of signifiers that impart significance not only through their consensual meaning, but also their shape on the page has been studied by Michel Foucault in *Les mots et les choses*. According to Foucault, Cervantes's *Don Quijote* expresses a radical epistemological change in the Western conception of signs. For Foucault, "[Don Quichotte]... est lui-même à la ressemblance des signes. Long graphisme maigre comme une lettre, il vient d'échapper tout droit du bâillement des livres. Tout son être n'est que langage, texte, feuillets imprimés... c'est de l'écriture errant dans le monde parmi les ressemblances des choses" (60).

9. Besides *La cifra impar*, Antin made two more adaptations of short stories by Cortázar. In 1962, he shot *Circe*, based on the short story of the same name. Despite their distance (Cortázar was in Paris, while Antin lived in Buenos Aires), both artists worked closely together. Cortázar wrote most of the dialogues in accordance with Antin's filmscript. In 1964, Antin made *Intimidad de los parques*, based on Cortázar's "Continuidad del los parques" and "El ídolo de las Cíccladas."

10. To this day, there have been twenty-one adaptations of Cortázar's texts: In 1962, after Antin's *La cifra impar*, Osías Wilensky produced *El perseguidor*, based on the short story of the same name. In 1963, Antin adapted *Circe* and in 1964, he produced his third adaptation of texts by Cortázar, *Intimidad de los parques*. In 1966, Italian director Michelangelo Antonioni shot *Blow-Up*, a free interpretation of Cortázar's "Las babas del diablo." Other adaptations are Jean-Luc Godard's *Week-end* (1967, a free adaptation of "La autopista del sur"), Walter Renaud's *La fin du jeu* (1971, on "Final del juego"), Claude Chabrol's *Monsieur Bébé* (1974), Luigi Comencini's *L'ingorgo (una storia impossibile)* (1978, on "La autopista del sur"), Miguel Picazo's *Cartas de mamá* (1978), José Antonio Páramo's *Instrucciones para John Howell* (1982), Michelle Bjornson's *End of the Game* (1988, on "Final del juego"). In 1994, Czech director Vytautas Palsis shot *Avtobus* (on "Ómnibus"), followed by Liz Hughes's short film *House Taken Over* (1997, on "Casa tomada"), Jana Bokovas's *Diario para un cuento* [1998]. In 1999, four films were made, based on short stories by Cortázar: Robert Cerendelli's short film *Instrucciones para subir una escalera*, Alexandre Aja's *Furia* (on "Graffiti"), Zhanna Kleimann's *Fear of Alternative Realities*, and Harriet Marin's short film *La nuit face au ciel* (both on "La noche boca arriba"). In 2005 Brazilian Roberto Gervitz presented *Jogo subterrâneo* (based on "Manuscrito hallado en un bolsillo"). The to-date last translation of a Cortázar text is Argentinean Diego Sabanés's *Mentiras piadosas* from 2008 (inspired by Cortázar's "La salud de los enfermos") [1966]. For further information on the films, see "Filmes basados en Julio Cortázar y en su obra": <http://www.juliocortazar.com.ar/archivo.htm>.

11. The use of these devices is also an important characteristic of many French films from the *Nouvelle Vague* movement of the 1960s. Antin has even been criticized for having copied from those films (unjustly, since his films are prior to the French ones). Paula Félix-Didier elaborates: "Para traducir la complicada estructura narrativa del cuento, Antin convirtió el relato epistolar [I do not consider "Cartas de mamá" an epistolary story] en una compleja estructura de *flashbacks* que se entrecruzan con el tiempo real de los personajes. Ese tratamiento le valió el calificativo de 'europeizante' y las acusaciones—tanto aquí [en la Argentina] como en Europa—de imitar cierto estilo de la *nouvelle vague* francesa, en especial al Alain Resnais de *Hiroshima mon amour* o *Hace un año en Marienbad*. De cualquier manera es significativo tener en cuenta que la literatura de Cortázar y el cine de Resnais tienen mucho en común, especialmente en el modo de relacionarse con el tiempo como una categoría que no es externa y dada sino relativa e interior" (8).

In an interview with María Lyda Canoso, Antin clarifies that he had not even seen Resnais's films until a year after the filming of *La cifra impar* (Cortázar, "*Cartas de cine*" 27).

12. The film critic of the Argentinean newspaper *Clarín* also highlights the atmospheric quality, but does not attribute it to any technical features: "La literatura de Cortázar… es una literatura de atmósfera… *La cifra impar* quiere ser testimonio de [eso]… El pasado… no es un tiempo puesto entre paréntesis, sino uno de los rostros del presente" (Cortázar, "*Cartas de cine*" 46).

13. Strangely enough, none of the printed or electronic material I consulted mentions Picazo as the director of *Cartas de mamá*. The WorldCat search engine lists Julio Sempere as the director of the film. Sempere, however, is responsible for the artistic effects. The opening and closing credits of the film prove to be the only source of verification.

14. As in *El hombre de la esquina rosada* the music in *Cartas de mamá* is from the Argentinean tango composer José Nieto.

15. Cortázar refers to Antin's *Los venerables todos*. A few years later, Antin adapted his text to the screen.

Chapter Four
Echoes in the Dark: *Pedro Páramo* on the Page and on the Screen

1. The subtitle characterizes *El gallo de oro* as a filmscript, and in fact, it has been adapted to the screen: in 1964 (even before the text had been published) by Roberto Gavaldón and in 1987 by Arturo Ripstein. However, this generic definition is limiting. *El gallo de oro* is a hybrid text that contains narrative, cinematic, and poetic elements. For further reference, see Alberto Vital's *Juan Rulfo* (52–53).

2. These studies are Gustavo Fares's *Imaginar Comala—El espacio en la obra de Juan Rulfo*, Marina Martín's "Espacio urbano y espacio psíquico en Juan Rulfo," and to some extent Edmundo Valadés's introduction to *Juan Rulfo: un mosaico crítico*, Katalin Kulin's *En busca de un presente infinito: Faulkner, Onetti, Rulfo y García Márquez*, and Liliana Befumo Boschi's "*Pedro Páramo* o el regreso al hombre."

3. Comala is not only Rulfo's fictive creation. There exists a Comala in the Mexican state of Colima.

4. This inversion is also expressed in the names and the functions of certain characters in the novel: the Catholic saints Pedro, Miguel, and San Juan are transformed into egotistical and exploiting figures: Miguel Páramo is a villain, his father Pedro Páramo is the tyrant of Comala who will end up destroying it, and Bartolomé San Juan abuses his own daughter.

5. Fabienne Bradu elaborates on the importance of the verb *sentir* in Rulfo's novel: "*Sentir* es un verbo que aparece en muchos… pasajes de la novela para definir las percepciones de los muertos o de los que están en tránsito hacia la muerte. … Sentir, para los muertos, se definirá como una diseminación de la percepción" ("La frase rulfiana" 77; emphasis in original).

6. Here, I disagree with Gustavo C. Fares, who, in *Imaginar Comala—El espacio en la obra de Juan Rulfo*, states: "Juan Rulfo es al espacio lo que Abundio es a Pedro Páramo: el hijo liberador… Rulfo hace con el espacio heredado de la Revolución Mexicana y de la tradición criollista lo que Abundio, el hijo natural del cacique Páramo, hace a su padre: lo elimina, lo deja hecho un montón de fragmentos. La acción del arriero es calificada como parricidio; la de Rulfo, podría llamarse espacidio?" (13). I do not interpret Abundio's assassination as a liberating act. Pedro Páramo has been passive and mourning long before he is killed. His death is not described as a liberation for Comala, as Fares reads it. Although the novella ends with the parricide, this is no real ending: Comala's time is not chronological. Its beginning narrates an event that is posterior to its ending. The place is still described as "hell," long after the despot has passed away. In addition, Abundio, the murderer of the father, tells Juan at the beginning of the narration that their father is still present, as a living bile.

7. The text has been adapted to the radio twice, once in Spanish, released in Mexico, and another in French, in Switzerland (Campbell 39–41).

8. To this date, there have been nine adaptations of Rulfo's texts: In 1955, Alfredo B. Crevenna filmed *Talpa,* followed in 1960 by Antonio Reynoso's *El despojo* (Rulfo wrote the script for this film), Roberto Gavaldón's *El gallo de oro* (1964, the screenplay was a joint venture of Juan Rulfo, Gabriel García Márquez, Carlos Fuentes, and Roberto Gavaldón), Rubén Gámez's *La fórmula secreta* (1964), Carlos Velo's *Pedro Páramo* (1966), Alberto Isaac's *El rincón de las vírgenes,* based on Rulfo's "Anacleto Morones" and "El día del derrumbe" (1972), François Reichenbach's *N'entends-tu pas les chiens aboyer?,* based on Rulfo's "¿No oyes ladrar los perros?" (1974), José Bolaños's *Pedro Páramo* (1976), and finally José Luis Serrato's *El hombre* (1978). For a detailed list of adaptations of Rulfo's texts and his own participation in films, as a screenwriter and actor, see the endnotes in Rulfo's *El gallo de oro y otros textos para cine* (131–34) and "Filmografía de Juan Rulfo" <http://www.sololiteratura.com/rul/rulfilmografia.htm>.

9. Velo inserts the different frames in the filmic narration according to a recurrent scheme: A character is talking to Juan Preciado, and either hears a sound that is reminiscent of a past situation or sees another character. Departing from this sudden remembrance, while the character starts to tell the traveler about the remembered situation, the screen shows a flashback of it.

10. The patron's dictum "la tierra no tiene divisiones" (103, 107) is a subversion of the motto of the Mexican Revolution, the demand of land and freedom, of "tierra y libertad."

11. There is also a melody that is played when Dolores appears on the scene or when her son, Juan Preciado, remembers her or hears her voice. Compared to this "Dolores" melody in a minor key, Susana's piece of music, in a major key, is much more joyful.

Chapter Five
Toward *Amor Vacui:* Gabriel García Márquez's and Ruy Guerra's *Eréndiras*

1. For an analysis of space in *El coronel no tiene quien le escriba* (*No One Writes to the Colonel*), *La mala hora* (*In Evil Hour*), *Cien años de soledad* (*One Hundred Years of Solitude*) and *Crónica de una muerte anunciada* (*Chronicle of a Death Foretold*), see Mario Vargas-Llosa's "García Márques: From Aracataca to Macondo."

2. In his biography on García Márquez, Dasso Saldívar refers to the story as follows: "La historia que más lo conmovería fue la de la anónima y escuálida niña a quien, según García Márquez, conoció por estos lares [*sic*]… [Fue] explotada de forma inclemente por una matrona que él imaginaría como 'su abuela desalmada' en uno de sus relatos más célebres… Al escritor [su memoria] le iba durar toda la vida…: primero lo perseguiría a través de las páginas de *Cien años de soledad,* luego buscaría acomodo en un guión cinematográfico y finalmente hallaría su propio espacio novelesco en 'La increíble y triste historia de la cándida Eréndira y de su abuela desalmada'" (263–64).

3. In the third chapter of the novel, Aureliano Buendía meets a young, nameless prostitute, whose fate is highly similar to Eréndira's: "Dos años antes, muy lejos de allí, se había quedado dormida sin apagar la vela… Desde entonces la abuela la llevaba de pueblo en pueblo, acostándola por 20 centavos para pagarse el valor de la casa incendiada" (García Márquez, *Cien* 145–46).

4. Arnold M. Penuel reads the short story as an allegoric portrayal of Spain's colonization of its American colonies: "Eréndira's illegitimacy serves as a vague pretext [for the grandmother's exploitation]. Her status as the younger Amadis' bastard daughter resembles the inferior status of the Indians as well as that of the colonies *vis-à-vis* the mother country, a fundamental condition of their exploitation… The story suggests that whatever idealistic reasons Spaniards, and historians may have advanced for Spain's conquest and colonization of the New World, the most important driving force and the one that shaped the country's relations with its colonies was the profit motive. The colonial relations provided an opportunity for maximum exploitation with minimal economic, legal, and moral constraints" (92–93).

This argumentation is to a large extent convincing, especially if one takes into account the role of the church in the short story and in the historic enterprise of the colonization. My only reservation regarding this interpretation is that the grandmother herself had been abused in her youth: She had been a prostitute, until Amadís (his name echoing the chivalric tale *Amadís de Gaula*, one of the favorite works of fiction of the Spanish *conquistadores*) freed her from the brothel where she had been trapped. I therefore read the grandmother's procedure as a re-enactment of the strategies of the Spanish conquerors.

5. In an interview, García Márquez states that "en Eréndira la imagen original [es la de] un burdel ambulante… había una cola mucho más grande que las otras… era una muchachita de no más de once o doce años" (Kaiserkern 216).

6. Readers of García Márquez's later fiction might remember the importance of the main square in *Crónica de una muerte anunciada*. The young Santiago Nasar, who has become the scapegoat of the collective rage, is executed at the very heart of the town. For an analysis of the space in this text, see Thomas Elsaesser's "Hyper-, Retro- or Counter-Cinema: European Cinema and Third World Cinema between Hollywood and Art Cinema."

7. Amy Katz Kaminsky, in "Women Writing about Prostitutes: Amalia Jamilis and Luisa Valenzuela," describes the prostitute as a placeholder of the male subject's desire: "The prostitute is called on to become any feminine type her customer requires" (119). Simone de Beauvoir, in *The Second Sex*, portrays her to be "necessary in so far as she remains an Idea into which man projects his own transcendence… but inauspicious as an objective reality" (186).

8. Some magical elements in the short story are reminiscent of the fictional universe in folk stories, such as the fact that Ulises turns glass into different colors or the telepathy between the lovers. Also, the grandmother has seemed to possess a superhuman power to survive the doses of rat poison, or the explosion of her piano while she was playing it. When she dies, her blood is not red, but green, like the blood of a dragon. For a detailed analysis on the motifs that are similar to the patterns of traditional fairy tales, see Jasbir Jain's "'Innocent Eréndira': The Reversal of a Fairy Tale," in the anthology *García Márquez.*

9. García Márquez's relation to cinema has been studied extensively. Among the most detailed analyses are Pedro Sorela's *El otro García Márquez. Los años difíciles*; Babette Kaiserkern's *Carlos Fuentes, Gabriel García Márquez und der Film. Kritische Untersuchung zu Geschichte und Phänomenologie des Films in der Literatur*; and Eduardo García Aguilar's *García Márquez: la tentación cinematográfica.* On the author's "temptation" of the other medium, García Aguilar notes: "El joven reportero de *El Espectador* se convertiría en el mejor cronista de cine de su época en Bogotá, luego estudiaría una temporada en el Centro Experimental de Roma… Después de un recurso frustrante, de 1961 y 1965, dedicado a hacer guiones… volverá al *cine perfecto* o sea la novela y escribiría *Cien años de soledad…* Después… intentará nuevas empresas cinematográficas. Por ejemplo asistiría… a los rodajes de *La viuda de Montiel*, de Littin y de *Eréndira*, de Ruy Guerra" (12–13).

10. Guerra is primarily known for his innovative work in Brazil's *Cinema Novo* movement of the 1960s and 70s. He made his directional debut with *Os cafajestes* (*The Unscrupulous Ones*, 1962), one of the movement's few mainstream successes. Up to today, he has directed twenty-two films; many of them are literary adaptations. In addition to directing, Guerra has also worked as an editor, producer, and actor and frequently co-wrote the films he directed. After Mozambique was decolonized, Guerra returned to his homeland to help the newly created national film institute, where he made *Mueda* (1979), the country's first feature film. His latest films are *Portugal S.A.* (2004), *In Evil Hour* (2005, an adaptation of García Márquez's novel *La mala hora*) and *The House of Sand* (2005). For a biographical account see *Le "Cinema novo* [*sic*] *" brésilien* (80–123).

11. The opening and closing credits are in French. All dialogues in the film are in Spanish.

12. In *Travels in Hyperreality*, Umberto Eco described a real space that has been fictionalized, the castle of William Randolph Hearst (which had become famous as the Xanadu of Orson Welles's *Citizen Kane*) that is highly similar to the description and showing of the grandmother's house: "Hearst… built his own Fortress of Solitude, which a biographer has described as a combination of palace and museum such as had not been seen since the days of the Medicis… The striking aspect of the whole is not the quantity of antique pieces plundered from half of Europe, or the nonchalance with which the artificial tissue seamlessly connects fake and genuine, but rather the sense of fullness, the obsessive determination not to leave a single space that doesn't suggest something… [it is] haunted by *horror vacui.* The insane abundance makes the place unlivable" (21).

13. The refrain of the grandmother's song, "j'ai laissé là mes jours innocents," foreshadows the granddaughter's fate.

Works Cited

Acosta, Marta. "Borges and Bertolucci: Two Conceptions of the Traitor and the Hero. *Lucero* 4 (1993): 65–69.

Agheana, Ion. "El Aleph." *Conversaciones sobre Borges.* Ed. Carlos Cañeque. Barcelona: Destino, 1999. 141–86.

Alazraki, Jaime. *Hacia Cortázar: aproximaciones a su obra.* Barcelona: Anthropos, 1994.

Alonso, Carlos J. Introd. "To Burn Like This without Surcease…" *Julio Cortázar—New Readings.* New York: Cambridge UP, 1998. 1–18.

El ángel exterminador. Dir. Luis Buñuel. Perf. Antonio Brave, César del Campo, Silvia Pinal, and Enrique Rambal. Criterion Pictures, 1962. Film.

Aragon, Louis. *Le paysan de Paris.* Paris: Gallimard, 1953.

Arlt, Roberto. *Los siete locos.* Buenos Aires: Losada, 1997.

Arrivée d'un train à la Ciotat. Dir. Auguste and Louis Lumière. 1895. Film.

"atopic." *Webster's Third New International Dictionary.* 2002.

Augé, Marc. *Non-lieux: Introduction à une anthropologie de la surmodernité.* Paris: Seuil, 1992.

Bal, Mieke. "Dispersing the Gaze: Focalization." *Looking In—The Art of Viewing.* Amsterdam: G and B Arts International Imprint, 2001. 41–63.

———. *Reading "Rembrandt": Beyond the Word-Image Opposition.* New York: Cambridge UP, 1991.

Barth, John. "The Literature of Exhaustion." *The Atlantic* 220 (1967): 29–34.

Barthes, Roland. *Fragments d'un discours amoureux.* Seuil: Paris, 1977.

Beauvoir, Simone de. *The Second Sex.* New York: Vintage, 1989.

Beckett, Samuel. *The Collected Shorter Plays.* New York: Grove, 2010.

———. *Happy Days, a Play in Two Acts.* New York: Grove, 2010.

———. *Waiting for Godot and Endgame.* New York: St. Martin's, 1992.

Befumo Boschi, Liliana. "*Pedro Páramo* o el regreso al hombre." *Rulfo: la soledad creadora.* Ed. Liliana Befumo Boschi and Violeta Peralta. Buenos Aires: Fernando García Cambeiro, 1975. 89–96.

———. *La problemática del espacio en la novela hispanoamericana.* Entre Ríos, Arg.: Mirador, 1984.

Bell-Villada, Gene. *Borges and His Fiction. A Guide to His Mind and Art.* Austin: U of Texas P, 1999.

———. *García Márquez: The Man and His Work.* Chapel Hill: U of North Carolina P, 1990.

Benjamin, Walter. *Illuminations.* Trans. Harry Zohn. New York: Harcourt, Brace & World, 1968.

Bhabha, Homi K, ed. *Nation and Narration.* New York: Routledge, 1990.

Blanchot, Maurice. *L'espace littéraire.* Paris: Gallimard, 1968.

Block de Behar, Lisa. "The Place of the Library." *Latin American Literary Review* 29 (2001): 59–75.

Bochner, Salomon. "Space." *Dictionary of the History of Ideas.* New York: Scribner's, 1974.

Bolongaro, Eugenio. "Why Truth Matters: Ideology and Ethics in Bertolucci's *The Spider's Stratagem.*" *Italian Culture* 23 (2005): 71–96.

Borges, Jorge Luis. *Collected Fictions, Jorge Luis Borges.* Trans. Andrew Hurley. New York: Penguin, 1989.

———. *Obras completas I. 1923–1949.* Buenos Aires: Emecé, 1996.

———. *Obras completas II. 1952–1972.* Buenos Aires: Emecé, 1997.

———. *Œuvres complètes I, II.* Ed. Jean Pierre Bernès. Paris: Gallimard, 1993 and 1999.

Bradu, Fabienne. *Ecos de Páramo.* Mexico City: Fondo de Cultura Económica, 1989.

———. "La frase rulfiana." *Juan Rulfo: un mosaico crítico.* Ed. Edmundo Valadés. Mexico City: Universidad Nacional Autónoma de México, 1988. 72–84.

Brecht, Bertolt. *Der Dreigroschenprozeß. Versuche 1–12.* Frankfurt: Suhrkamp, 1959.

Brüggemann, Heinz. *Das andere Fenster: Einblicke in Häuser und Menschen. Zur Literaturgeschichte einer urbanen Wahrnehmungsform.* Frankfurt a. M.: Fischer, 1989.

Bynum, Caroline Walker. *Metamorphosis and Identity.* New York: Zone Books, 2001.

Calderón de la Barca, Pedro. *La vida es sueño.* Madrid: Austral, 1998.

Campbell, Federico. "En el país de la impunidad, Pedro Páramo es el rey." *Juan Rulfo: un mosaico crítico.* Ed. Edmundo Valadés. Mexico City: Universidad Nacional Autónoma de México, 1988. 39–46.

Cañeque, Carlos, ed. *Conversaciones sobre Borges.* Barcelona: Destino, 1999.

Cartas de mamá. Dir. Miguel Picazo. Perf. Guillermo Gentile, Susana Mara, Julio Núñez, and Mercedes Segura. Films for the Humanities and Sciences, 1978. Film.

Certeau, Michel de. *L'invention du quotidien—I. Arts de faire.* Paris: Gallimard, 1990.

Chatman, Seymour. *Story and Discourse: Narrative Structure in Fiction and Film.* Ithaca: Cornell UP, 1978.

La cifra impar. Dir. Manuel Antin. Perf. María Rosa Gallo, Maurice Jouvet, Sergio Renán, and Milagros de la Vega. Norma Vigo, 1962. Film.

Le "Cinema nôvo [sic]" brésilien (1). Ed. Michel Estève. Paris: Minard, 1972.

Corner, James. "The Agency of Mapping: Speculation, Critique and Invention." *Mappings*. Ed. Dennis E. Cosgrove, London: Reaktion, 1999. 213–52.

Cortázar, Julio. *Buenos Aires, Buenos Aires*. Photo. Sara Facio and Alicia D'Amicio. Buenos Aires: Sudamericana, 1983.

———. *Cartas 1937–1963*. Vol.1. Ed. Aurora Bernárdez. Buenos Aires: Alfaguara, 2000.

———. *"Cartas de cine" de Julio Cortázar a Manuel Antin*. Ed. María Lyda Canoso. Buenos Aires: n.p., 1995.

———. *Obras completas*. Vols. 1 and 3. Introd. Saúl Yurkiévich. Barcelona. Galaxía Gutenberg, 2003–04.

———. *Territorios*. Mexico City: Siglo Veintiuno, 1978.

Cozarinsky, Edgardo. *Borges in/and/on Film*. New York: Lumen, 1988.

Deleuze, Gilles. *Cinéma 1: L'image-mouvement*. Paris: Minuit, 1983.

———. *Cinéma 2: L'image-temps*. Paris: Minuit, 1985.

Deleuze, Gilles, and Félix Guattari. *Capitalisme et schizophrénie—Mille plateaux*. Paris: Minuit, 1980.

Derrida, Jacques. *La dissémination*. Paris: Seuil, 1972.

———. *Sauf le nom*. Paris: Galilée, 1993.

Deveny, Thomas G. *Contemporary Spanish Film from Fiction*. Lanham: Scarecrow, 1999.

Un diccionario de films argentinos. Ed. Raúl Manrupe and María Alejandra Portela. Buenos Aires: Corregidor, 1995.

Diccionario del cine español. Ed. José Luis Borau. Madrid: Alianza, 1998.

Echavarría, Arturo. *El arte de la jardinería china en Borges y otros estudios*. Madrid: Iberoamericana, 2006.

Eco, Umberto. *Travels in Hyperreality: Essays*. San Diego: Harcourt Brace Jovanovich, 1986.

Elsaesser, Thomas. "Hyper-, Retro- or Counter-Cinema: European Cinema and Third World Cinema between Hollywood and Art Cinema." *Mediating Two Worlds: Cinematic Encounters in the Americas*. London: British Film Institute, 1993. 119–38.

Eng, David L., and David Kazanjian, eds. *Loss: The Politics of Mourning*. Berkeley: U of California P, 2003.

Eréndira. Dir. Ruy Guerra. Perf. Michael Lonsdale, Claudia Ohana, and Irene Papas. Les Films du Triangle, 1982. Film.

Ernst, Christoph. "Gespenst, Phantom, Wiedergänger. Zur medienphilosophischen Lektüre der Dekonstruktion." *Perspektiven interdisziplinärer Medienphilosophie.* Ed. Christoph Ernst, Petra Gropp, and Karl Anton Sprengard. Bielefeld: Transkript, 2000. 45–68.

Estrada Cárdenas, Alba Sovietina. *Estructuras y discurso de género en "Pedro Páramo" de Juan Rulfo.* Mexico City: Universidad Michoacana de San Nicolás de Hidalgo, 2005.

Fares, Gustavo C. *Imaginar Comala—El espacio en la obra de Juan Rulfo.* New York: Peter Lang, 1991.

Félix-Didier, Paula. "Cortázar, cazador de crepúsculos." *Film* 10 (1994): 6–11.

Fernández Ferrer, Antonio. "Estrategias de la araña (de Borges a Bertolucci)." *Borges. Un'eredità letteraria.* Ed. Pia Masiero. Venice: Università Ca'Forscari di Venezia, 2008. 37–58.

Filmes basados en Cortázar y en su obra. N.p., n.d. Web. 19 Nov. 2011. <http://www.juliocortazar.com.ar/archivo.htm>.

Filmografía de Juan Rulfo. 1 Oct. 2010. N.p., n.d. Web. 19 Nov. 2011. <http://www.sololiteratura.com/rul/rulfilmografia.htm>.

Foucault, Michel. "Des espaces autres." *Dits et écrits 1954–1988.* Paris: Gallimard, 1994. 752–62.

———. *Les mots et les choses.* Paris: Gallimard, 1966.

———. *Surveiller et punir. Naissance de la prison.* Paris: Gallimard, 1975.

Foucault, Michel, and Michel Blanchot. *La pensée du dehors.* Paris: Fata Morgana, 1986.

Franco, Jean. *Critical Passions: Selected Essays.* Durham: Duke UP, 1999.

Freud, Sigmund. "Mourning and Melancholia." *The Standard Edition of the Complete Psychological Works of Sigmund Freud.* Vol. 14. London: Hogarth, 1955. 239–60.

Fuguet, Alberto. *Las películas de mi vida.* Madrid: Alfaguara, 2003.

García Aguilar, Eduardo. *García Márquez: la tentación cinematográfica.* Mexico City: Filmoteca UNAM, 1985.

García Lorca, Federico. *Obras completas.* Vol. 2. Madrid: Aguilar, 1955.

García Márquez, Gabriel. *Cien años de soledad.* Madrid: Cátedra, 2004.

———. *La increíble y triste historia de la cándida Eréndira y de su abuela desalmada: siete cuentos.* Buenos Aires: Sudamericana, 1972.

Gass, William H. "A True Lie-Minded Man." *The American Novel since World War II.* Ed. Marcus Klein. Greenwich: Fawcett, 1969. 262–70.

Haverkamp, Anselm. "The Memory of Pictures: Roland Barthes and Augustine on Photography." *Comparative Literature* 45.3 (1993): 258–74.

Hombre de la esquina rosada. Dir. René Mugica. Perf. Susana Campos, Jacinto Herrera, Francisco Petrone, and Walter Vidarte. Argentina Sono Film, 1962. Film.

El hombre de la esquina rosada. Dir. Miguel Picazo. Perf. Susana Mara, Lautaro Murúa, Jaime Nero, and Gogo Rojo. Radiotelevisión Española, 1961. Film.

Iser, Wolfgang. "The Reading Process: A Phenomenological Approach." *Reader-Response Criticism: From Formalism to Post-Structuralism.* Ed. Jane P. Tompkins. Baltimore: John Hopkins UP, 1994. 50–96.

Jain, Jasbir: "'Innocent Eréndira': The Reversal of a Fairy Tale." *García Márquez.* Ed. John Fiddian. New York: Longman, 1995. 197–203.

Jameson, Fredric. "Of Islands and Trenches: Neutralization and the Production of Utopian Discourse." *Diacritics: A Review of Contemporary Criticism* 7.2 (1977): 2–21.

———. *Postmodernism, or The Cultural Logic of Late Capitalism.* Durham: Duke UP, 1991.

Jauß, Hans Robert. *Literaturgeschichte als Provokation.* Frankfurt a. M.: Suhrkamp, 1970.

Jowett, Benjamin. Introduction to *The Republic* by Plato. Trans. Jowett. *The Internet Classics Archive* by Daniel C. Stevenson. MIT. Web. 2 Oct. 2010. <http://classics.mit.edu/Plato/republic.1.introduction.html>.

Kaiserkern, Babette. *Carlos Fuentes, Gabriel García Márquez und der Film. Kritische Untersuchung zur Geschichte und Phänomenologie des Films in der Literatur.* Frankfurt a. M.: Peter Lang, 1995.

Kaminsky, Amy Katz. "Women Writing about Prostitutes: Amalia Jamilis and Luisa Valenzuela." *The Image of the Prostitute in Modern Literature.* New York: Frederick Ungar, 1984.

Kant, Immanuel. *Critique of Practical Reason and Other Writings in Moral Philosophy.* Trans. Lewis White Beck. Chicago: U of Chicago P, 1950.

Kestner, Joseph. "Secondary Illusion: The Novel and the Spatial Arts." *Spatial Form in Narrative.* Ed. Jeffrey R. Smitten and Ann Daghistany. Ithaca: Cornell UP, 1981. 100–28.

Kino-(Ro)Mania—Intermedialität zwischen Film und Literatur. Ed. Jochen Mecke and Volker Roloff. Tübingen: Stauffenberg, 1999.

Kirby, Kathleen. *Indifferent Boundaries: Spatial Concepts of Human Subjectivity.* New York: Guilford, 1996.

Kling, Sylvia. *Filmologie und Intermedialität—Der filmologische Beitrag zu einem aktuellen medienwissenschaftlichen Konzept.* Tübingen: Stauffenberg, 1999.

Kloepfer, Rolf. "Intertextualität und Intermedialität oder die Rückkehr zum dialogischen Prinzip. Bachtins Theoreme als Grundlage für Literatur- und Filmtheorie." *Kino-(Ro)Mania—Intermedialität zwischen Film und Literatur.* Ed. Jochen Mecke and Volker Roloff. Tübingen: Stauffenberg, 1999. 23–46.

Koenigsberg, Ira. "The Art of Technology: Contours of Space in the Science Fiction Film." *Space and Beyond: The Frontier Theme in Science Fiction.* Westport, CT: Greenwood, 2000.

Kristeva, Julia. *Le texte du roman.* La Hague: Mouton, 1970.

Kulin, Katalin. *En busca de un presente infinito: Faulkner, Onetti, Rulfo y García Márquez.* La Habana: Artes y Literatura, 1987.

Lacan, Jacques. Écrits: *A Selection.* New York: Northon, 1977.

Lefebvre, Henri. *La production de l'espace.* Paris: Anthropos, 1974.

Léonard, Jacques. "L'historien et le philosophe: A propos de *Surveiller et punir; Naissance de la prison.*" *L'impossible prison: Recherches sur le système pénitentiaire au XIXe siècle. Débat avec Michel Foucault.* Ed. Michelle Perrot. Paris: Seuil, 1980. 9–28.

Lewis, Daniel K. *The History of Argentina.* Westport, CT: Greenwood, 2001.

Literatur intermedial. Musik, Malerei, Photographie, Film. Ed. Peter V. Zima. Darmstadt: Wissenschaftliche Buchgesellschaft, 1995.

Little, Christopher. "*Eréndira* in the Middle Ages: The Medievalness of Gabriel García Márquez." *García Márquez.* Ed. John Fiddian. New York: Longman, 1995. 204–13.

Leyshon, Andrew, David Matless, and George Revill. Introd. "Music, Space, and the Production of Place." *The Place of Music.* Ed. Leyshon, Matless, and Revill. New York: Guilford, 1998. 1–30.

Martín, Marina. "Espacio urbano y espacio psíquico en Juan Rulfo." *Revista Hispánica Moderna* 54 (2001): 126–39.

Martínez Andrade, María. "Espacio e identidad en tres relatos de Borges." *Borges: Nuevas lecturas.* Ed. Juana Alcira Arancibia. Buenos Aires: Corregidor, 2001. 189–99.

Marting, Diane E. "The End of Eréndira's Prostitution." *Hispanic Review* 69 (2001): 175–90.

Matteo, Sante. "History as a Web of Fictions: Plato, Borges, and Bertolucci." *Weber Studies: An Interdisciplinary Journal* 6 (1989): 12–29.

McFarlane, Brian. *Novel to Film: An Introduction to the Theory of Adaptation.* Oxford: Clarendon, 1996.

McMurray, George R. *Gabriel García Márquez.* New York: Frederick Ungar, 1977.

Medientheorie. Medienwissenschaft. Aufsätze—Personen—Grundbegriffe. Ed. Helmut Schanze. Stuttgart: Metzler, 2002.

"Medium." *Oxford English Dictionary.* 2nd ed. 1993. Web.

Méndez, José Luis. *Como leer a García Márquez. Una interpretación sociológica.* Río Piedras: Editorial de la Universidad de Puerto Rico, 1989.

Moran, Dominic. *Questions of the Liminal in the Fiction of Julio Cortázar.* Oxford: U of Oxford P, 2000.

More, Thomas. *Utopia.* Introd. David Harris Sacks. Boston: Bedford, 1999.

New Jerusalem Bible. Ed. Susan Jones. New York: Doubleday, 1985.

Onetti, Juan Carlos. *El pozo.* Madrid: Seix Barral, 1979.

Ortega y Gasset, José. *La deshumanización del arte y otros ensayos de estética.* Madrid: Revista de Occidente, 1987.

Oubiña, David. *Manuel Antin. Los directores del cine argentino.* Buenos Aires: Centro Editor de America Latina, 1994.

Paech, Joachim. "Artwork-Text-Medium: Steps en Route to Intermediality." 19 Nov. 2011. <http://www.unikonstanz.de/FuF/Philo/LitWiss/MedienWiss/Texte/interm.html>.

Pedro Páramo. Dir. Carlos Velo. Perf. Narciso Busquets, Carlos Fernández, John Gavin, and Pilar Pellicier. Clasa Films Mundiales and Producciones Barbachano Ponce, 1966. Film.

Pedro Páramo. El hombre de la Media Luna. Dir. José Bolaños. Perf. Blanca Guerra, Manuel Ojeda, Bruno Rey, and Patricia Reyes Spíndola. Conacine, 1976. Film.

Penuel, Arnold M. *Intertextuality in García Márquez.* York, SC: Spanish Literature Publication, 1994.

Perspektiven interdisziplinärer Medienphilosophie. Ed. Christoph Ernst, Petra Gropp, and Karl Anton Sprengard. Bielefeld: Transcript, 2000.

Picon Garfield, Evelyn. *¿Es Julio Cortázar un surrealista?* Madrid: Gredos, 1975.

Plato, and T.D.J. Chappell. *The Plato Reader.* Edinburgh: Edinburgh UP, 1996.

Poe, Edgar Allan. *Tales of Mystery and Imagination.* London: J. M. Dent, 1912.

Psarra, Sophia. "'The Book and the Labyrinth Were One and the Same'—Narrative and Architecture in Borges' Fictions." *Journal of Architecture* 8.3 (Sept. 2003): 369–91.

Richardson, Bill. "Spatial and Deictic Reference in Three Borges Stories." *A Lifetime's Reading: Hispanic Essays for Patrick Gallagher.* Ed. Don W. Cruickshank. Dublin: U College Dublin P, 1999. 166–83.

Robbe-Grillet, Alain. *Instantanés*. Paris: Minuit, 1962.

Rodríguez Monegal, Emir, ed., introd., notes. *Jorge Luis Borges: Ficcionario. Una antología de sus textos*. By Jorge Luis Borges. Mexico City: Fondo Económico de Cultura, 1981.

———. Interview with Carlos Cañeque. *Conversaciones sobre Borges*. Ed. Carlos Cañeque. Barcelona: Destino, 1999. 21–44.

Roemer, Kenneth M. *Utopian Audiences—How Readers Locate Nowhere*. Amherst: U of Massachusetts P, 2004.

Rulfo, Juan. *Biografía armada*. Ed. Reina Roffé. Buenos Aires: Corregidor, 1973.

———. *El gallo de oro y otros textos para cine*. Mexico City: Era, 1980.

———. *Obra completa*. Carácas: Ayacucho, 1977.

———. *Pedro Páramo*. Madrid: Cátedra, 2002.

———. "*Pedro Páramo*, treinta años después." *Cuadernos Hispanoamericanos* 421 (1985): 5–7.

Sábato, Ernesto. *Sobre héroes y tumbas*. Buenos Aires: Ayacucho, 2004.

Sabugo Abril, Amancio. "Comala o una lectura en el infierno." *Cuadernos Hispanoamericanos* 421 (1985): 417–32.

Saldívar, Dasso. *García Márquez: El viaje a la semilla. La biografía*. Madrid: Alfaguara, 1997.

Sánchez, Luis Rafael. *La guaracha del Macho Camacho*. Buenos Aires: Flor, 2001.

Sánchez, Marta. "A View from Inside the Fishbowl: Julio Cortázar's 'Axolotl.'" *Bridges to Fantasy*. Ed. George Edgar Slusser, Eric S. Rabkin, and Robert E. Scholes. Carbondale: Southern Illinois UP, 1982. 38–50.

Santos-Phillips, Eva. "Power of the Body in the Novela *The Incredible and Sad Tale of Innocent Eréndira and of [sic] Her Heartless Grandmother*." *Literature Film Quarterly* 31.2 (2003): 118–23.

Scafi, Alessandro. "Mapping Eden: Cartographies of the Earthly Paradise." *Mappings*. Ed. Dennis E. Cosgrove. London: Reaktion, 1999. 52–68.

Schwartz, Marcy E. "Cortázar Under Exposure: Photography and Fiction in the City." *Latin American Literature and Mass Media*. Ed. Edmundo Paz-Soldán and Debra A. Castillo. New York: Garland, 2001. 117–38.

Segal, Charles. "Ovid's Metamorphic Bodies: Art, Gender and Violence in the Metamorphoses." *Arion* 5 (1997): 9–41.

Shaw, Donald L. *Borges' Narrative Strategies*. Liverpool: Francis Cairns, 1992.

Sorela, Pedro. *El otro García Márquez: Los años difíciles.* Madrid: Mondadori, 1988.

Spivak, Gayatri, Chakravorty. "Can the Subaltern Speak?" in: *Colonial Discourse and Post-Colonial Theory: A Reader*. Ed. Laura Chrisman and Patrick Williams. New York: Columbia UP, 1994. 66–111.

———. *The Spivak Reader: Selected Works of Gayatri Chakravorty Spivak.* Ed. Donna Landry and Gerald MacLean. New York: Routledge, 1996.

Stadler, Eva Maria. "Bresson, Dostoevsky, Bakhtin: Adaptation as Intertextual Dialogue." *Quarterly Review of Film & Video* 20 (2003): 15–22.

Stam Robert. *Film Theory: An Introduction.* Malden: Blackwell, 2000.

———. *Literature through Film: Realism, Magic, and the Art of Adaptation.* Malden: Blackwell, 2004.

Strategia del ragno. Dir. Bernardo Bertolucci, Perf. Giulio Brogi, Franco Giovanelli, Alida Valli. Radiotelevisione Italiana, 1970. Film.

"Tara." *Encyclopedia Britannica Online.* Encyclopedia Britannica, 2010. Web. 1 Oct. 2010.

Tcherepashenets, Nataly. *Place and Displacement in the Narrative World of Jorge Luis Borges and Julio Cortázar.* New York: Peter Lang, 2008.

Tower Sargent, Lyman. "Utopianism." Def. *Routledge Encyclopedia of Philosophy*. London: Routledge, 2000. Web.

"Translation." *Webster's Third New International Dictionary*. 2002.

Urrutia, Jorge. *Imago litterae: cine, literatura.* Sevilla: Alfar, 1984.

Valadés, Edmundo, ed. and introd. *Juan Rulfo: un mosaico crítico*. Mexico City: Universidad Nacional Autónoma de México, 1988.

Vargas-Llosa, Mario. "García Márquez. From Aracataca to Macondo." *Gabriel García Márquez.* Ed. Harold Bloom. New York: Chelsea House, 1989. 5–20.

Virilio, Paul. *Essai sur l'Insécurité du territoire.* Paris: Stock, 1976.

———. *A Landscape of Events.* Cambridge, MA: MIT P, 2000.

Vital, Alberto. *Juan Rulfo*. Mexico City: Consejo Nacional para la Cultura y las Artes, 1998.

Wicks, Ulrich. "Borges, Bertolucci, and Metafiction." *Narrative Strategies: Original Essays in Film and Prose Fiction*. Ed. Syndy Conger, Janice R. Welsch. Malcomb: Western Illinois University Library, 1981. 19–36.

Yurkiévich, Saúl. "Nueva refutación del cosmos." *Revista Iberoamericana* 41 (1975): 3–14.

Index

About the Book and the Author

Some of the most important writers of the twentieth century, including Borges, Cortázar, Rulfo, and García Márquez, have explored ambiguous sites of a disquieting nature. Their characters face merging perspectives, deferral, darkness, or emptiness. Such a space is neither a site of projection (as *utopia* or *dystopia*) nor a neutral setting (as the *topos*). For the characters, it is real and active, at once elusive and transforming. Despite the challenges of visualizing such slippery spaces, filmic experimentations in Spanish American cinema since the 1960s have sought to adapt these texts to the screen. Ilka Kressner's *Sites of Disquiet* examines these representations of alternative dimensions in Spanish American short narratives and their transformations to the cinematic screen. The study is informed by contemporary critical approaches to spatiality, especially the concepts of *atopos* (non-space), spaces of mobility, sites of *différance*, of a self-effacing presence, and sonic spaces.

Kressner's comparative study of textual and cinematic constructions of non-spaces highlights the potential and limits of interarts adaptation. Film not only portrays the sites in ways that are intrinsic to the medium, but during the cinematic translation, it further develops the textual presentations of space. Text and film illuminate each other in their renderings of echoes, gaps, absences, and radical openness. The shared focus of the two media on precarious spaces highlights their awareness of the physical and situational conditions in the works. Therefore, it vindicates the import of space and dwelling, and the often underestimated impact of surroundings on the human body and mind. Despite their heterogeneity, the artistic elaborations of these ambivalent *atopoi* all share a liberating impulse: they assert creative and open-ended interactions with space where volatility ceases to be a negative term.

Ilka Kressner, the University at Albany, State University of New York, focuses on twentieth-century to contemporary Spanish American literature and arts, often from a comparative perspective. Her research interests include intermediality (word, image, sound), notions of space in art (encompassing the related topics of vertigo, free fall, and velocity), ecocriticism, and aesthetics of interaction.